LET'S GET REAL

A realistic approach to investing in property in any market

REVISED EDITION

Luke Harris

MAJOR STREET

'Three things cannot be long hidden:
the sun, the moon, and the truth.'

Buddha

First edition published in 2018 by Major Street Publishing Pty Ltd.
This second edition published in 2023.
info@majorstreet.com.au | +61 421 707 983 | majorstreet.com.au

© Luke Harris 2023
The moral rights of the author have been asserted.

 A catalogue record for this book is available from the National Library of Australia

Printed book ISBN: 978-1-922611-83-3
Ebook ISBN: 978-1-922611-84-0

All rights reserved. Except as permitted under *The Australian Copyright Act 1968* (for example, a fair dealing for the purposes of study, research, criticism or review), no part of this book may be reproduced, stored in a retrieval system, communicated or transmitted in any form or by any means without prior written permission. All inquiries should be made to the publisher.

Cover design by Simone Geary
Internal design by Production Works
Illustrations by Paul Lennon
Printed in Australia by Griffin Press

10 9 8 7 6 5 4 3 2 1

Disclaimer: The material in this publication is in the nature of general comment only, and neither purports nor intends to be advice. Readers should not act on the basis of any matter in this publication without considering (and if appropriate taking) professional advice with due regard to their own particular circumstances. The author and publisher expressly disclaim all and any liability to any person, whether a purchaser of this publication or not, in respect of anything and the consequences of anything done or omitted to be done by any such person in reliance, whether whole or partial, upon the whole or any part of the contents of this publication.

Contents

Welcome **1**
Meet the author **3**

PART I | PREPARE TO GET REAL 9

Chapter 1	Why the *why* matters	**11**
Chapter 2	Rediscovering your why!	**19**
Chapter 3	Are you ready for it?	**26**
Chapter 4	How badly do you want it?	**33**
Chapter 5	What type of investor are you?	**38**
Chapter 6	All investors have something to fear	**51**
Chapter 7	Speculating vs investing	**60**
Chapter 8	Out of the hot tub and into a bigger and better one!	**65**
Chapter 9	Are we there yet?	**76**
Chapter 10	Good things take time	**82**
Chapter 11	Is it time?	**86**

PART II | IT'S ALL ABOUT YOU 99

Chapter 12	Do you mind if we discuss your mindset?	**101**
Chapter 13	She'll be right, mate…	**108**
Chapter 14	Planning your road map to success	**114**
Chapter 15	Defining your Point B	**123**
Chapter 16	A mentor will help you stay on track	**129**
Chapter 17	Your three Ds	**138**
Chapter 18	Flying to the moon on your own?	**150**

PART III | WHY PROPERTY? 159

Chapter 19   So why invest in property at all? **161**
Chapter 20   House price stability **169**
Chapter 21   Population growth **183**
Chapter 22   Property – it's where the money is **188**
Chapter 23   The ability to add value **196**
Chapter 24   There is more than one way to pat the proverbial property cat! **200**
Chapter 25   Where to now? **216**

Can The Property Mentors help you? **222**

Welcome

By reading this book you will be able to learn from my two decades' experience in business, property and investing. I am the founder of arguably Australia's most trusted and respected property mentoring service, The Property Mentors. From humble beginnings, with little experience and nothing more than big dreams and a can-do attitude, I have created and continue to grow significant wealth through property for clients and for myself.

This book is not designed to show you a cookie-cutter approach to finding investment riches. No, I have specifically written this book to help you get clear on exactly what you want to achieve from your investing and in your life, and to provide you with proven systems that I have used to achieve exceptional results in property.

You see, we all have dreams, desires and goals for our lives, and they are different for each of us. There is no single right way, or 100% guaranteed approach, to achieve all your goals. But with the right planning and the right people in your corner, you can take control of your own destiny. And if you are up for the challenge, I am confident that you too can learn to succeed in the property game.

I trust you will enjoy this book and the new perspective you will have when you have finished reading it.

Meet the author

Even as a young lad growing up in suburban Perth, Luke was always entrepreneurial, looking for creative ways to make money. He did the paper round from age ten, sold raffle tickets for schools and sports clubs and even put his mum and dad's kitchen utensils out on a blanket on the street to sell them off. (His mum has some great stories about that!) Luke's entrepreneurial spirit came directly from his parents, who both taught him that you can do whatever you want in life if you put your mind to it. However, they probably hadn't meant Luke to take it quite so literally!

At age 12, Luke remembers seeing the hard rubbish piled up in the street ready for collection and wondering why people would throw out perfectly good stuff. So, he spent hours dragging it back to his parents' garage and storing it up until the next local swap-meet. Luke's dad has many stories about Luke waking him up at 5 o'clock on Sunday mornings to drop him off with a trailer-load of 'goods' to sell!

As far as Luke was concerned it was like money for jam – what a great business model!

Luke had big dreams. His dad was a high-level marathon runner and he taught Luke a valuable lesson in life: if you're going to do something, do it right the first time. Although he didn't realise it at the time, Luke learned a lot from observing his dad and he continues to use these life lessons every day.

At age 14, Luke saw an opportunity to work in a 'real' job and started doing three-hour shifts at Hungry Jack's. While other kids his age had never even thought about getting a job, Luke was out there earning money and saving for one of his big goals, which was to buy a video camera. He stuck the video camera advertisement on his bedroom wall and worked his butt off until he eventually saved up enough money to buy one. Even though he hated maths classes in school, Luke ran an income and expenses book where he would track his every cent (money he spent buying lollies and movie tickets and money he received at Christmas from relatives) so that he always knew his financial position. When he had a goal, he worked backwards from it and realised that he had to get serious if he was going to achieve it.

At age 16, Luke was introduced to the network marketing business Amway, where he learned a wealth of information that wasn't being taught at school. He learned that there was more to life than just going to work and getting a pay packet and that working for yourself had the potential to generate huge profits. The training Amway provided introduced Luke to the importance of having the right mindset and dreaming big. He was rubbing shoulders with successful Amway representatives who had replaced their regular incomes with income streams they were making through the system, and these people didn't judge him on his age. They offered their full support – unlike some of his school teachers, who weren't as encouraging. Luke ultimately realised, though, that network marketing was not something he could get super passionate about.

Luke didn't enjoy school either, so he wrote letters to more than 80 local electricians asking for an apprenticeship. With only one interview and no job offer, it was clear that his mass-marketing approach wasn't working. He then spoke to the careers coordinator at his high school and expressed an interest in leaving school and asked for help. Not long after, an opportunity came up to work in the electronic security industry as a trainee alarm installer. He jumped at the chance! After almost a year in his first full-time job, Luke realised that he was not going to progress far in that organisation. So, with some experience behind him and his dedicated work ethic, he applied for roles at other security companies and was offered a role as an installer for a larger firm. Not long after that, a position came up in the office where Luke could get off the tools and be involved with the management team. This is where he learned about the internal workings of a business. By age 18, Luke had increased his income every year but once again found himself in a role where his income-earning potential was capped. So, he asked his boss if he could become a subcontractor on the weekends to earn some extra money. He learned pretty fast that he could earn the same on weekends as he could working all week – and, better still, he had the luxury of choosing which jobs were scheduled for him!

A young entrepreneur

Between the ages of 19 and 23, Luke established and ran his own electronic security business in Perth, which generated great revenues. By this time, Luke was eager to buy property, but the banks did not see lending to self-employed people as attractive as lending to PAYG salary-earners, so he learned first-hand how bank lending policies could affect his ability to grow a portfolio. Eventually, Luke was able to secure a loan and at age 20 he had bought his very first property.

With his eyes firmly fixed on building a property portfolio, even at this early stage in life, he sold his security business so he could continue to invest. He then took a PAYG job in Sydney to continue building wealth through property. After 13 months in Sydney, his obvious talents and work ethic were recognised by his new employer, who offered him the opportunity to relocate to Melbourne to open their new state office. Six months into that gig, Luke saw opportunities for the business that the owners simply weren't taking up. So, to avoid missing out on what he saw as a huge opportunity, Luke left that company and, armed with more knowledge and experience, he started his second security firm in 2005, quickly growing that business into an even bigger success than his first.

A fresh start

At age 30, Luke sold his second business and was – so he thought – ready to retire. Despite the banks' lending policies, he had continued to build a sizeable property portfolio while running his businesses, and with the sale of his second business he had plenty of cash.

So, he relocated to Perth to be close to his loved ones (and to enjoy some warmer weather), and he went on a series of extended overseas trips throughout Europe, South America and Asia. This 18-month 'mini retirement' was a huge learning and growth period for him, during which time he was able to refocus on what he truly wanted out of life.

During his twenties, Luke had built up a multi-million-dollar property portfolio and performed numerous renovations, land subdivisions and unit developments. He had bought off the plan, invested in mining towns and basically tried every property strategy under the sun to build wealth – not too different to a lot of other investors out there, really!

While he had clearly been able to achieve healthy results, he knew deep down that he could have done it so much better. Luke had also helped dozens of friends and family members make money from property, quite literally setting some of them up for life! (And keep in mind, this was all without any formal training, just a genuine desire to help others and a passion for property.)

The birth of The Property Mentors

Contemplating his next move, Luke decided to relocate back to Melbourne in November 2011, where he fulfilled a long-term property goal to own a direct beachfront property. Luke moved in, spending the next 12 months – and a huge chunk of cash – turning this property into a high-quality home. He still owns this property and it continues to generate a solid rental return for all his efforts.

By now, Luke had decided that his never-ending passion for property had to be turned into a proper business. He started formulating the steps required to professionally mentor people on their property investing journeys.

Luke spent a lot of time analysing exactly what makes investors tick and worked out why most investors never achieve the results they desire. While there is a lot of money to be made in property, most investors just don't know how to do it properly. Luke also spent time and energy stripping back the entire property investment industry, assessing exactly what works and what doesn't from a client perspective.

In early 2014 he made the decision to establish a highly ethical, education-focused, long-term mentoring business known today as The Property Mentors.

PART I

PREPARE TO GET REAL

Let's Get Real combines the experience of decades of personal and business property investing that I have gained over the years – and the learnings from years of trial and error – to build systems that almost any investor can follow to dramatically improve their results.

I look forward to sharing my knowledge with you in this book. Now, if you feel that you are ready, *Let's Get Real*!

Chapter 1

Why the *why* matters

'There are two great days in a person's life – the day we are born and the day we discover why.'

William Barclay

First, congratulations for picking up a copy of this book. By doing so, I assume that you want better results in your life than you are enjoying right now. Deep down, you probably also know that you need some help to achieve your life goals, even if you don't exactly know what those goals are or what that help might look like just yet.

If you've just read the 'Meet the author' section, you will know that I have been investing in property and businesses for over 20 years. I now manage a property portfolio worth tens of millions of dollars. I progressed beyond simply learning about investing, and I committed to getting real-world, practical results in the property space. Despite my success, though, I am still learning and perfecting my craft. In fact, I will never stop learning.

I have worked now with thousands of investors, at all levels, and have turned my passion for property into a successful business that is focused on one thing: helping other investors, just like you, to get the type of results they really desire.

> **Mentor tip**
> The quality of your life will be determined by the quality of the questions you ask of yourself and others.

I don't do this by telling you what to do. Instead, I help you to focus on your ambitions by asking better questions.

You see, if you don't ask yourself great questions, how can you ever expect to get great answers?

The first question I asked myself when I first decided to establish The Property Mentors was: if I were to start over on my own investment journey, what type of property education, mentoring, support and opportunities would I want to have access to?'

Then I used WHY questions to help create the essential frameworks of HOW I would run the business:

- Why help other people invest? What are my emotional rewards in doing so?
- Why choose property as a major part of any wealth plan?
- Why not just keep all this knowledge to myself?

The whole basis for my business – and probably the largest part of its success – has stemmed from WHY I set it up in the first place.

Mentoring others to success was the answer

After achieving some pretty impressive results personally, I fell into the role of mentoring my friends and family. The emotional rewards I gained by helping others get ahead in life remain one of my key drivers today. There is nothing more satisfying than helping someone get ahead in life – financially and emotionally. So, when the demand for the type of help I was able to provide became impossible to ignore, I decided to establish The Property Mentors.

I continued to ask questions:

- What is good about the property investment industry?
- What is wrong with the property investment industry?
- What was missing in the property investment industry?
- How can I add something of high value to the property investment industry?

I didn't ask myself, 'How can the business make lots of money?' or 'What do people want to hear?' My purpose was, and always will be, to genuinely add value to people's lives. So instead, when I was establishing the rules of how the business would operate, I asked, 'Where can I provide the most value?' and 'What do people really need to be successful property investors?'

For the record, The Property Mentors is not just another property company. We do not consider ourselves to be either property 'bulls' or property 'bears'. We know that you can make money in both good times and bad – and there are strategies for both. Property is just a tool and, if it is used well, it can help you to achieve amazing results. Our approach focuses less on property and more on YOU and the type of investor you ultimately want to become.

Let's Get Real

> 'The truth that makes men free is for the most part the truth which men prefer not to hear.'
>
> Herbert Agar

Like most things I do in the investing space, the choice of title for my book *Let's Get Real* was purposeful and considered. The aim of the title is to hopefully get you to pause for a moment and reflect on your situation. Are all the things you are currently doing, or not doing, helping you to live the type of lifestyle you really desire?

You see, one of the most challenging things we can do as human beings is to truly confront our own results in life.

In other words, I start with YOU.

Throughout this book, you will see #LetsGetReal when I want you to stop and think and be conscious of the point I am making. #LetsGetReal is my way of highlighting a home truth, or something I consider vitally important. When you see #LetsGetReal, I want you to read over that part again and stop and think about the message conveyed so you can really start to process the learnings behind it.

I am going to ask you questions and challenge you to think about how you got to be where you are today, as well as where you want to get to in the future. Some people may tend to want to skip over this emotional work. They may find it uncomfortable to answer the questions I am going to ask.

But since I am going to ask you to get real with me, it is only fair that I also get real with you.

Like most investors, I started my investment journey with only a small amount of capital and some big dreams. And, like most investors, I made most, if not all, of the common mistakes the vast majority of investors continue to make today. I was the victim of my own lack of education. I didn't know exactly what to do back then, so I attended seminars and events, took part in online webinars, read books, property magazines and newspapers and watched DVDs to try and increase my knowledge.

Because I did not have a clear plan of why (the emotional drivers), or how (the strategic planning) to invest, I just jumped from opportunity to opportunity. I was guilty of chasing the next big thing or trying to fast-track my way to wealth and, at times, I was blind to what was most important and what I ultimately wanted to achieve.

Over the course of my own investment journey, I have learned that money will flow from the uneducated (or undereducated) to the educated and from the impatient to the patient – or from those who don't have a clear plan to those who do. The property industry has more than its fair share of 'sharks' and 'cowboys' who are only too happy to liberate you from your hard-earned savings in order to make a quick buck for themselves.

You can think of money as a magnifier of human behaviour. Good people with more money can do more good in the world and vice versa. Unfortunately, though, the pursuit of money will often bring out the worst in mankind. And I have seen the good, the bad and the downright ugly in the property industry. Throughout this book, I will not be afraid to expose those bad and ugly elements, and show you plenty of the good stuff in the process!

Why I wrote this book

Despite those limitations, like many people investing in property in Australia over the last 20 years, I still managed to make healthy profits from my decision to invest in property. But, in the spirit of getting real, I admit that a large chunk of the early wealth I created was probably a result of just being in the game, rather than being a master of it.

If I was given the chance to go back and start my investment journey over again with the knowledge, experience and systems I have today, I can only speculate on how much better my results could have been. It is not just about the extra wealth that I could have created but, more importantly, the time, stress and heartache I could have avoided.

And that is why I wrote this book. My aim is to provide you with a chance to learn from my mistakes, to benefit from my wisdom, to fast-track your results and ultimately to help you enjoy a higher quality of life without having to do it all on your own.

When I started planning this book, I continued to ask questions such as:

- How is this book going to benefit the lives of anyone who reads it?
- What unique perspective am I able to bring to my readers?
- If I were only ever going to read one more book on property investing, what would it look like?

By naming this book *Let's Get Real*, I hope to differentiate it from all the other property investing 'how-to' guides that already line the bookshelves. I encourage you to think of this book as more of a 'why-to' guide, because a large part of your investment success does not come down to a lack of access to technical information but rather a lack of planning and tactical execution.

I could bombard you with all the practical 'how-to' knowledge – and my company, The Property Mentors, provides members with high-quality, practical instructions on property research, negotiation and access to expert accounting, tax planning, finance and so on – but the effect of that information is terminally limited if you don't take the time and do the work upfront to adequately address the reasons WHY you are investing.

This book follows the growth journey and the exact same systems that I use personally and that we now teach our members at The Property Mentors. There is a logical order that any investor must follow to achieve the best results, and this book will guide you through that pathway chapter by chapter.

Whether you are new to investing or have been investing for some time, you may be tempted to jump straight into some of the more practical how-to sections in the latter part of this book. However, this book is designed to build your knowledge chapter by chapter, and if for any reason you were only going to read half of this book, I would strongly recommend that you read the first half. It is in the first half that I really get into the things that hold most investors back. These are the emotional roadblocks — many of which you are probably blissfully unaware of — that, if you leave them unaddressed, will forever limit your results.

Finally, this book is designed to explain, not to replace, all the systems and processes that our mentors go through with our members one-on-one at The Property Mentors. As you read through this book, you are going to come to the conclusion either that what we do resonates with you or that it doesn't. If it does and you choose to continue on this journey with us, then it becomes our mission to help you achieve all your dreams, goals and desires more safely, more quickly and more predictably than if you were to simply go it alone.

> 'If you want to build a ship, don't drum up people together to collect wood and don't assign them tasks and work, but rather teach them to long for the endless immensity of the sea.'
>
> Antoine de Saint-Exupéry

At some stage, you are probably going to have one of those aha moments when you say to yourself:

- That really makes sense!
- These guys know what they're doing.
- They have my back and genuinely want me to succeed in life.
- There is a win-win value proposition for me if I continue to work with them in the longer term.

#LetsGetReal

This process is not for the faint of heart. *Let's Get Real* has the potential to dramatically change your results and transform your life, but only if you immerse yourself in the process and get real — not only with me but, most importantly, with yourself.

So, with all of that said, let's get into what I believe will have the biggest impacts on your investment results and your life.

I am going to ask for your permission to mentor you to achieve the types of results that most people crave but fail to achieve. In doing so, there is a very real possibility that you will find certain elements of this process somewhat uncomfortable.

I am going to ask you to get real with yourself and be accountable for all your results – both good and bad – in the past, the present and, most importantly, into the future.

So, before we dive in, do I have your permission to mentor you through this process?

Are you sure?

Well, if you are ready, let's get real and let's get started!

Chapter 2

Rediscovering your why!

'When we're born, we want to know why the stars shine. We want to know why the sun rises.'

Michio Kaku

When we were young, we wanted to know everything. We probably drove our parents mad. If you are a parent with young children now, you'll know that their intrinsic curiosity can be a source of wonder and, at times, yes, exasperation.

'Why is the sky blue, Mummy?'

'It just *is*, okay? Now shoosh, please, and just eat your breakfast.'

At some point in life, for many of us, that natural curiosity sadly stopped or faded away over time as other priorities took over. Perhaps we just got sick of our parents' exhausted attempts to explain all the wonders of the universe to us. Or perhaps the joy of learning got beaten out of us when we were forced to rote-learn our ABCs or times tables at school.

Anyway, at some point in our lives we stop being curious and asking questions, especially the types of questions that are difficult or uncomfortable to answer. Luckily for you, that's what this book is all about – asking the tough questions, those that most people are too afraid to ask – because at the end of the day, if we don't ask them, who will?

Any time we start talking about a person's core beliefs, what they really hold dear, things can get emotional. Things can get real! But you have to look inwards if you want real, lasting impact from this process.

This book is as much about the process of self-discovery as about investment success because the two are inextricably linked. It is a process where I will guide you to peel back all the parts of yourself, layer by layer, to find out whether they are helping you get closer to your goals in life or holding you back from achieving all of your life dreams, goals and desires.

Are you ready?

> 'You can never cross the ocean unless you have the courage to lose sight of the shore.'
> *Christopher Columbus*

So again, do I have your permission to mentor you and get real with you? Are you open to being real with me? Before you jump in with a reflexive if somewhat apprehensive 'yes!', I want you to really think about how open you are prepared to be and how far you are willing to go in this process. Are you willing to dive straight in, or to only get your toes wet?

Throughout this book, I will use a series of stories, illustrations and case studies to highlight some key points, starting with this little analogy.

Imagine you were standing on one side of a lake and your goal was to get to the other side. Now, if you knew your goal was to get to the other side of the lake, and it was vitally important that you got to the other side, how would you approach it?

Would you edge your way down to the shoreline, dip one toe in the water and then remove it quickly because the water was cold? Perhaps you would build up the courage to put both feet into the water and maybe even walk out as far as your knees. You know you want to get to the other side of the lake, so you push yourself to get out as deep as your waist. It's cold, you are uncomfortable and the safety of the shoreline is just behind you; it wouldn't take much to go back.

Maybe this goal of getting to the other side of the lake isn't so important after all... Doubt creeps in. Your discomfort builds. You begin to have second thoughts and start to question why you are doing this, but by now you are already up to your chest and you eventually say 'bugger it' and start swimming towards the other side of the lake.

Now, contrast this with an alternate approach. You simply run to the edge and dive straight in and start swimming towards the other side of the lake.

Which approach is better? In both cases, the goal is to get to the other side of the lake. In both cases, you are going to get wet and uncomfortable and there is going to be plenty of work to do to get to the other side. So, surely the best approach is to get to the middle of the lake as quickly and painlessly as possible, right?

Why did we focus on the middle of the lake? Because once you reach the middle, it's just as easy to keep going as it is to turn around.

When it comes to change, in our opinion, there are two pathways that you can take. The first is to resist it, kicking and screaming the whole time, until you eventually give in to the change. The second is that you embrace the change and jump in head-first to enact the change as quickly as possible.

Intellectually, you probably agree it is a better strategy to just dive into the lake and start swimming.

We tell ourselves that it is common sense not to drag out the inevitable and to get the result we want sooner. However, common sense is not commonly practised, because as human beings we are first and foremost emotional creatures – our emotional selves will often override our logical selves.

> **#LetsGetReal**
> It is our emotions that dictate WHY we do most of the things that we do in life.

This is WHY I have written this book – to give you a chance to learn about your emotional self and master many of the emotions that are holding you back from achieving all your intellectual goals.

So, are you ready to dive into the lake with me? Great! (I knew you would say yes!)

> **Mentor tip**
> Learning about how you make emotional decisions in life is one of the first steps to taking back control of your destiny.

There's always a risk

Investing in property can be an incredibly lucrative wealth-creation strategy. Then again, although there are many upsides, there is still the potential for you to lose everything if you get it wrong. It's a cruel, cruel world out there and there are a lot of nasty surprises that you can, and most likely will, encounter throughout your property investing journey.

> 'Risk comes from not knowing what you're doing.'
> *Warren Buffett*

Risk in any investment always lies with the investor. If you lose money, it's usually your fault because you chose to invest.

Does that sound a bit harsh? Like it or not, it's the simple truth – I am not here to sugar-coat anything.

It is usually possible to achieve the financial results you want without taking unnecessary risks, or being excessively greedy, or for someone else to lose in order for you to win. But, in case you hadn't worked this out by now, nobody is going to build a successful property portfolio for you. At some point you need to take responsibility for your investing. There are people out there who will help you to get that result, but the ultimate responsibility lies with you.

You need to do your research and understand the risks before signing anything, or paying anything; that way, even if you do lose money, you won't be blaming anyone but yourself.

To become a successful property investor in Australia, you need a solid commitment to achieve the results you desire. There is no easy pathway to success and you will have to overcome some huge challenges on your journey – this applies no matter what you want to achieve in life.

Mentor tip
Success is a little like a game of golf. You need to have a whole bag of different clubs at your disposal to cope with any situation you find yourself in when you're out on the course.

Every investor is different and, therefore, what works for one investor could turn out to be a total disaster for another. The majority of property investors in Australia only ever own one investment property, but it seems *everyone* is an expert on the topic.

The average investor often makes huge financial decisions with very little technical knowledge about the property market, how it works and how to build and grow a successful portfolio.

Most investors do not take the time to work through the processes outlined in this book, which prepare them emotionally for investing in property. In my opinion, it is your emotional readiness that will determine at least 80% of your results.

> **#LetsGetReal**
>
> I am going to challenge you to think quite a bit. I am going to challenge you now to consider the *thought processes* you currently go through when you make decisions on a daily basis.

Why are you investing?

> 'It is good to have an end to journey toward;
> but it is the journey that matters, in the end.'
>
> Ursula K. Le Guin

How did you get to where you are right now in your life? What choices, decisions, beliefs and actions (or inactions) have contributed to the total of your results to date? Thinking about your answers to these questions will give you greater insight into how you make investment decisions.

Let's Get Real is not intended to be a happy, feel-good, 'warm and fuzzy' book that makes you believe everything is rosy. It has been written to show you how to get your successful property portfolio well underway, how to keep it and how to live the life you desire as a planned result, not through luck. It will also teach you about YOU as an investor.

You may feel a little uncomfortable at times as you find out what sort of investor you are. Bear with me through any discomfort and remind yourself that it's actually a good thing because it means you are open to growing. Whether you have no investment properties or dozens of properties, there is *always* another level to your investing. No matter how successful you consider yourself to be, there is always more to learn and you can always improve. The property market is a cheeky beast. The way you invested 5, 10 or 20 years ago may not apply in today's or tomorrow's market.

There is a saying that you've probably heard before: 'You can't see the forest for the trees'. But what does that actually mean?

Well, it means that we often get so caught up in our own lives, and the minutiae of our daily existence, that we forget to step back and take a look at the big picture. At The Property Mentors, we encourage all our members to regularly imagine themselves jumping into a helicopter and zooming up above their day-to-day lives, then looking down at what they are currently doing to get ahead financially. I encourage you to do the same now. Ask yourself, 'Is all that I am currently doing really getting me the results I want?' If you're reading this book, I'm guessing that the answer is 'no'. So, come with me as we look next at whether you're ready to take the steps to achieve financial freedom.

#LetsGetReal
Take this moment to think about the big picture. Why are you actually investing in the first place?

Chapter 3

Are you ready for it?

'It is what we think we know already that often prevents us from learning.'

Claude Bernard

I am going to make a big call now and tell you that all the information you could ever need to build wealth in property is already out there! Don't believe us? Just google 'property investment' and see how much information exists on the topic.

So, if all the information you could ever need is already out there, why isn't everyone already a mega successful property investor?

You see, relevance is everything when it comes to information. And that is where my skill as a mentor comes into play. I will help you to understand which pieces of information are relevant to you and your wealth plan. This is a skill that, when you acquire it, will be a powerful tool for change. Not only that, knowing how to apply relevant information is a skill even fewer possess.

If your fan belt needs replacing, you could google 'fix my car' and find millions of generic results. But if you are more specific and search for 'how to replace a fan belt on a 1996 Series 2 Holden VS Commodore', you will find more specific information. Although, even then, you may not know exactly which is the best way to fix your problem, let alone the most cost-effective or safest.

However, if you knew a mechanic who has worked on thousands of Holdens, he or she would undoubtedly be able to tell you immediately not only which fan belt to use but the best way to remove the old one and put on the new one. You might even be able to pay them to do the job for you to make sure it is done right. (That is called outsourcing, and I come back to the concept later in this book.)

In this example I would like to point out that most people don't fix their own cars these days, because it makes sense to outsource something so important to a professional. Given that investing your hard-earned dollars in property is a big deal, do you really want to take the risk of doing it all on your own?

Becoming financially free

'Financial freedom' is a term that is thrown around a lot in the property and investment industries. When was the last time you actually thought about what that means to you?

Take a moment to consider what it would be like to have complete financial freedom – not just being financially independent but being totally FREE. It's clearly a dream that many aspire to but few will ever achieve.

To get the best results, you must be ready to take on the responsibility, accountability and workload that is required to achieve your financial and life goals.

When it comes to investing, there are some fundamental truths that you can't shortcut. In fact, I have identified three levels of readiness that all investors will need to pass through if they really want to get the best results from their property investment journey. You simply can't bypass any of these levels if you want to be truly successful.

Level 1 - Emotional readiness

As humans we are often very good at wishing for a lot. We would all, no doubt, love to be millionaires and have financial freedom, or have better relationships, or enjoy our jobs more, or have better health, or... the list is endless.

The problem is that simply wishing for these things will not make them happen. What we are not so good at is becoming emotionally ready to say, 'Enough is enough'. Learning how to get to the point emotionally where you can draw a line in the sand and claim, 'From this day forward, I will... (insert whatever goal you are looking to accomplish here)' – and then actually put in the time, energy and effort to make it happen – is not easy.

The reason most investors never get to this level of emotional readiness is that they don't understand the process. They either haven't had the knowledge, invested the time or had a mentor to guide them through the process of discovering what their emotional needs are as an investor.

> **#LetsGetReal**
> We are all carrying emotional baggage. It's how you handle it that matters.

Don't feel special; we all carry emotional baggage – some more than others. Consider the following:

- Some of us doubt ourselves too much.
- Some of us overrate our skills and abilities.
- Some of us fear making a mistake and so make the mistake of doing nothing.
- Some of us have too much fear.
- Some of us will self-sabotage because we feel, due to whatever past indiscretions, that we are now not worthy of future success.

- Some of us believe that all the love, happiness and abundance that is available on the planet is reserved for someone else.

Or, to sum it up with a quote from Mike Myers' movie *Wayne's World*, 'We're not worthy'. There, I've said it. It's out in the open and, now that it is, let's find a way to become bridge builders… and get over it.

We often need to find strategies to push our emotions aside if we truly have the desire and goals to really change our results.

Now for a hard question: what sort of life do you actually deserve?

Wow! Talk about an in-your-face, confronting question! Dude!

Confronting this question will be integral to your success as a property investor – and it is an integral part of the mentoring process we go through one-on-one at The Property Mentors.

Becoming emotionally ready will often mean facing up to things such as:

- your inner demons
- self-defeating inner talk
- arrogance
- ego
- pride
- your sense of identity
- admitting that you DESERVE this success.

Confronting these challenges is about as deep and as real as it gets.

Mentor tip

While reading this book is no substitute for the one-on-one work we do with members at The Property Mentors, it is a way to make you bring these issues to the surface. The investment that we, as mentors, have to make into your lives can be profound. Not everyone is going to be ready to be emotionally honest with us and, quite often, with themselves.

Level 2 - Educational readiness

A lot of people are keen to jump the gun when it comes to investing. They just want to get out there and start investing – and learn on the job, so to speak. I am the first to admit that when I started out I probably jumped the gun all too often. I accept that at times I got seduced by the fast-talking spruikers with their big promises and suffered far too often from shiny-object syndrome. I jumped from one investment strategy to another without having a clear plan of why and how I should have been investing.

While this approach didn't kill me – and I learned many valuable (and costly) lessons along the way – if I had my time over again, I would do some things very differently.

If, after reading everything in this book, you still want to go out and take that approach, good luck to you. But smart people are willing to learn from the mistakes of others and take advantage of all the resources that are available to them.

> 'Education is a progressive discovery of our own ignorance.'
>
> *Will Durant*

With investing, your education must always come before your results. And that education will be incremental and ongoing. Only as you layer the theoretical principles with real-world practical experience can your education and your results rise to the next level.

#LetsGetReal

If I were to ask you on a scale of 0 to 10 – where 10 is you as an expert property investor making six or seven figures from your investments every year and 0 is you having no clue what you are doing – where would you honestly rate yourself right now? Now ask yourself where you would like to be. How big is that gap?

Over the years, we have developed some specific systems that can help you fill that gap between where you are right now and where you really need to be to achieve the type of results you desire. Filling that gap in the fastest and safest manner is not the sort of thing you can usually learn just by reading a book or watching a DVD or online video. The skill The Property Mentors has to take you from where you are today to where you really want to be financially is the culmination of years of personal investing, as well as helping thousands of other investors to achieve fantastic results over the years. As well as understanding the tools and education I can provide for you in this book, you will also need to go through the experience of learning these lessons in a practical way.

Level 3 - Financial readiness

Some of you may have your finances well under control, but many will need help to become financially ready to invest.

One of the problems for people struggling to get ahead financially is that they don't actually know where their money goes. It is a little bit like the mystery of the missing socks in the washing. You know what I mean? No matter how careful you are, somehow, mysteriously, a sock will go missing every few loads.

> 'If a man empties his purse into his head, no man can take it away from him. An investment in knowledge always pays the best interest.'
>
> Benjamin Franklin

Most people can tell me off the top of their head what their physical weight is to within a few kilograms. Far fewer can tell me their 'financial weight' to within a few hundred dollars. Why?

Good money management habits have nothing to do with how much income you earn. I have seen clients on huge incomes who are still living week to week and don't know how much money they have at their disposal at any point in time. I call these people 'money lazy'. They have high incomes and just assume that there will always be more money available in their next pay cheque, so there is nothing to worry about. However, many of these high-income earners work in high-risk professions such as mining, banking or IT, and so their job security is affected by the economic conditions of the day.

#LetsGetReal
Ask yourself this: if your current source of income dried up tomorrow, how long would your money last?

At the other end of the scale are the 'money fretters' who worry constantly about where the next dollar is coming from.

What both groups have in common is that they actually don't have a well-established money management program in place that can not only help them better manage their financial affairs but also cause them less stress.

With the help of appropriate professionals, you can become financially ready to invest. You'll learn to analyse your current levels of income, debt, equity and superannuation to determine what you can safely afford to invest with now and in the future.

Some of you may have to change your money management habits, and others may have to learn to create and stick to budgets to maximise the limited financial resources you have now.

Even if you have money for investment burning holes in your pockets, that does not mean you should be out there investing – at least not until all three levels of readiness have been addressed. Sometimes, as a mentor, I need to slow you down in the short term in order to speed you up over the longer term.

Next, I will ask how badly you want to achieve your goals.

Are you ready to answer?

Chapter 4

How badly do you want it?

> 'How different our lives are when we really know what is deeply important to us, and keeping that picture in mind, we manage ourselves each day to be and to do what really matters most.'
>
> *Stephen R. Covey*

Much of what I cover throughout this book is not sparkling, shiny and new. Some of it you may have heard before. In fact, while I have some amazing concepts and ideas to share with you, a lot of what I've written in this book has been around in one form or another for years, sometimes even for centuries. But, unlike ideas you find in many other books, I will endeavour to show you how these ideas are relevant to you and your investment journey.

> **Mentor tip**
> Learning how to apply information to your personal situation is more important than simply accessing information.

Let me introduce you now to ET, the Hip-Hop Preacher, Dr Eric Thomas, who shares a unique and powerful story called the

'Secret to Success' on YouTube. You can go and watch it online now, or I've paraphrased it here.

The story goes like this. There was once a young man who wanted to make a lot of money. So, he asked a wealthy old man, a guru, if he would teach him the secrets to becoming rich and successful.

He told the old man, 'You know, I wanna be on the same level you are', and the old man said, 'If you wanna be on the same level I'm on, then I'll meet you tomorrow at the beach at 4 a.m.'

The young man was keen, so he arrived dressed up in his best suit at 3.45 a.m., ready to learn how to make money.

The old man arrived promptly at 4 a.m. in a pair of boardshorts and he asked the young man, 'How badly do you wanna be successful?'

The young man replied, 'Real bad'.

So, the old man grabbed the young man by the hand and led him down the beach and into the water – suit and all.

Now the young man had all sorts of things running through his mind, like, 'Man, this old guy is crazy'. But they walked further out until the water was up to his waist. The young man said to himself, 'I wanna make money and he's got me out here swimming'.

Still the old man continued to lead the young man deeper until the water was at his shoulders. The young man was thinking, 'I didn't ask to be a lifeguard. I wanna make money, he's got me in here ruining my best suit'.

Still the old man pulled him further out until the water was up to the young man's mouth. The young man was thinking, 'I'm going to need to go back in, this guy is out of his mind'.

The old man, seeing the doubt in the young man's eyes, simply said, 'I thought you said you wanted to know the secrets to success'.

The young man bravely said, 'I do'.

So, the old man said, 'Then walk a little further'.

The young man continued until the old man grabbed his head and held it down under the water. The old man's strength belied his age and physical appearance as he held the young man down. The young man was fighting with everything he had to push his head back out of the water, but he was no match for the older man. The young man was thrashing and flailing about, and then, just before he was about to pass out, the old man raised him up and asked, 'You still want to know the secret?'

The young man meekly nodded, gasping for breath.

The old man said, 'Well, the secret is that, when you want to succeed as badly as you just wanted to breathe, then you will be successful'.

Obviously, this is just an illustrative fable. I am not going to ask you to meet me at the beach and try to drown you (unless, of course, that is what I need to do to help you really understand this lesson).

But if you tell me you want to become a really successful property investor and enjoy an amazing lifestyle, then I have to ask you, 'How badly do you want it?'

#LetsGetReal

How badly do you want to achieve property success? Is it that you sort of want it? Or that it would be nice to have it, and if it happens then great, but if it doesn't that's okay too? Or do you really want it?

As a mentor, it is my job to hold a mirror up in front of you. I am not here to judge you, just to help you get real with yourself. There are no right or wrong answers to the questions I ask you, only truth or lies. That's how you bring the relevance of the information home to roost.

So, let me ask you, what sort of desire are you bringing to this mentoring relationship?

Seriously, on a scale of 0 to 10 – where 0 is that you don't care and 10 is that you absolutely must have it – how important is it to you to build a multi-million-dollar property portfolio capable of providing you with the type of income you really want?

Be honest. What would you score yourself for desire?

___ / 10.

Are you okay with that score? Does something need to change?

Do you get it now? Do you understand that the level of your success in any area of your life will be a direct reflection of your level of desire?

How many examples of this principle can you recall from your own life experiences? When was the last time you were really hungry for something? Can you think of a time when you wouldn't take no for an answer? How did that affect your actions and results? Equally, can you remember some examples in your life when clearly your lack of desire led to some lacklustre results?

After desire comes action

But wait up, did any of you think, 'That's it? All that is missing from my life is simply a strong enough desire – end of story?'

No? Well, good, neither do I! Desire alone will rarely be enough. It needs to be coupled with appropriate and commensurate ACTION.

Now for the hard part. You have to make a big commitment to your results. You have to be willing to pay the price for that success upfront. You have to be willing to do the work before you get to enjoy the benefits.

> 'Vision without action is merely a dream.
> Action without vision just passes the time.
> Vision with action can change the world.'
>
> *Joel A. Barker*

To quote one of the greatest boxers to ever live, the late Muhammad Ali, 'The fight is won or lost far away from witnesses – behind the lines, in the gym and out there on the road, long before I dance under those lights... I hated every minute of training, but I said, "Don't quit. Suffer now and live the rest of your life as a champion"'.

> **#LetsGetReal**
> You have to be able to look at yourself in the mirror and say,
> 'I deserve to succeed because I am willing to do whatever it takes to make it'.

And, sure, you might have to fake it before you make it, and perhaps you won't even enjoy the process, but you have to know before you get started that you can't go into this half-arsed and expect to smash it.

Believe me when I say life is going to test your resolve. You are going to face many of life's challenges and many unforeseen obstacles before you make it. Life is going to test your energy, your patience and your skills before it hands over all its riches.

As a final thought for this chapter, are you willing to commit to the process of being a little smarter than yesterday, to work a little bit harder today, to become a little better tomorrow and take a more strategic approach to building the life you desire? If this sounds like you, then keep reading, because we are about to discover what type of investor you are.

> **Mentor tip**
> Little by little one gets far. Success takes sacrifice, dedication and commitment, but you can achieve your goals one step at a time.

Chapter 5

What type of investor are you?

'The only way you will ever permanently take control of your financial life is to dig deep and fix the root problem.'

Suze Orman

So far, I have asked you a few pertinent questions. I have asked you to think about why you want to become a property investor, whether you are ready to immerse yourself in the process of change and just how badly you want to succeed as a property investor.

Like you, many Australians love the idea of owning investment property. As property mentors, the biggest issue I see is how they go about making this happen.

Technically, the act of buying a property and renting it out makes you a property investor. But the term property 'investor' applies loosely in this situation.

You see, there is a huge difference between those who simply buy a property as an investment and professional property investors who have the necessary skills to achieve amazing results.

Table 1: Growth in number of property investors

Underlying data	2015–16		2016–17		2017–18		2018–19		2019–20	
	no.	$m	no.	$m	no.	$m	no.	$m	no.	$m
Rental income and deductions										
Gross rental income	2,087,468	42,139	2,149,796	44,145	2,201,414	46,345	2,220,007	47,834	2,253,520	48,846
Rental interest deductions	1,707,429	21,749	1,752,186	21,953	1,784,560	23,739	1,785,800	24,008	1,792,065	21,524
Capital works deductions	1,022,396	3,271	1,082,156	3,619	1,119,849	3,849	1,140,015	4,065	1,175,648	4,306
Other rental deductions	2,099,248	20,676	2,161,227	21,867	2,211,261	22,377	2,226,726	22,798	2,254,147	23,190
Net rental income	**2,116,755**	**-3,557**	**2,179,107**	**-3,294**	**2,229,520**	**-3,619**	**2,244,857**	**-3,036**	**2,270,911**	**-166**
Estimated resident population Australia	24,190,907		24,594,202		24,966,643		25,340,217		25,655,289	
Percentage of property investors	8.6%		8.7%		8.8%		8.8%		8.8%	

Source: Australian Taxation Office and Australian Bureau of Statistics

According to data from the Australian Taxation Office (ATO) and the Australian Bureau of Statistics (ABS) in Table 1, the number of individuals claiming rental income from their investment properties has risen from 2.087 million to 2.253 million. Over the same period, the total amount of rent received has risen from just over $42 billion to just under $49 billion a year.

However, as a percentage of the Australian estimated resident population (ERP) data published by the ABS, the percentage of people choosing to invest in Australian property over that period has been fairly steady at just under 9%, or just over 1 in 12 people.

If we dive deeper into the data (see Table 2), we see that the vast majority (over 90%) of Australian property investors only own one or two investment properties. Less than 1% of property investors own six or more properties. That's fewer than 20,000 Australians.

Table 2: Number of properties owned by investors

No. of property interests	2017–18	%	2018–19	%	2019–20	%
1	1,571,217	71.16	1,589,563	71.37	1,592,883	71.53
2	418,806	18.97	420,529	18.88	418,637	18.80
3	129,784	5.88	129,816	5.83	129,390	5.81
4	47,469	2.15	47,319	2.12	46,765	2.10
5	19,861	0.90	19,513	0.88	19,271	0.87
6+	20,756	0.94	20,434	0.92	19,895	0.89
Total	2,207,893		2,227,174		2,226,841	

Source: Australian Taxation Office

#LetsGetReal
There's a difference between buying a property and renting it out, and being a property investor. Less than 1% of rental property owners have a portfolio of six or more properties.

What type of property investor do you want to become?

It's important to define what type of property investor you are while also planning for the long term and deciding what kind of investor you want to become.

Before we can do this, I need to ask you some questions to get you thinking:

1. Are you looking for a small result or a big result from your investing efforts?
2. Are you looking to invest in property as a hobby or are you going to treat it as a professional business?

The answers to those two questions will determine how to proceed from here.

For example, when was the last time you looked at your financial situation and assessed where you are at in life? I am serious, guys and gals. When did you last look at all your figures – your investments, savings, superannuation, credit cards, loans, mortgages and so on – to work out exactly where you are in life from a financial perspective? Yesterday? A year ago? Five years ago? Never?

I meet thousands of investors and wannabe investors every year who have never, ever reviewed their financial situation or considered their strategy.

Am I serious? Yes… people actually laugh when I ask that, as if I am joking and know the punchline already. I don't see anything even slightly funny about this situation. In fact, it's quite scary that people can be so blasé about something that affects their life in such a massive way. Often, it's actually quite sad.

Surprisingly, it's not the stupid or unintelligent people who live in financial denial but everyday people – mums and dads, high-income-earning professionals, students, factory workers, even lawyers and pilots. There is no industry or profile that isn't represented here.

This continues to amaze me and was partly the reason I started The Property Mentors in the first place.

Investor profiles

If you are not already financially free then you most likely fit into one, or a combination, of the following investor types. I recognise that these categories are generalisations, but I would be surprised if you didn't recognise some parts of yourself, or the people you know, in one of the profiles.

The wannabe investor

The wannabe investor is always reading books, newspapers, magazines and internet forums and seems to be an expert among their family and friends, but somehow they still never seem to invest in anything much themselves. They have probably dabbled in some form of investing before and possibly still have a small holding of Telstra shares. They are very good at talking the talk. The wannabe investor might invest small amounts of money from time to time and likes to follow trends a lot. The wannabe investor is also the type who is most likely to fall for get-rich-quick schemes.

The pseudo confidence of the wannabe investor usually comes from a genuine interest in investing. However, they are often unable to pull the trigger themselves when it comes to putting their own money in the game. This may be because of fear, so they talk big but often fall well short of becoming true masters of the game.

Around other non-investors, they may come across as really knowledgeable, but when you look below the surface they are exposed simply as wannabe investors who lack any real results.

The frugal investor

If you invest, you are going to pay for your education one way or another. You can choose to pay upfront for education from a trusted source and for a fixed price – for example, you may have invested $29.99 in this book. You probably saw that it was reasonably priced and made the decision that an investment in the information contained within this book represented good value.

What you probably didn't know was that the information contained within these pages is the result of my investment experience of 20-plus years, which includes my investment in my own education of hundreds of thousands of real, hard-earned dollars. By purchasing this book, you are leveraging OPE (other people's experience) – that $$29.99 investment is starting to look even more valuable than you first thought!

Beyond this book, you may choose to become a member of The Property Mentors. If so, you will know how much we charge for mentoring for a specific period and you will know in advance exactly what that process will entail.

It is a simple enough equation: you pay X and you get Y in return. And, of course, you want Y to be higher, ideally much higher, than X.

However, the frugal investor doesn't want to invest anything into their education upfront. They will sign up for any and every investment seminar, webinar or course, but only if it is free. Unfortunately, a large proportion of the property industry is only too happy to oblige these people. Spruikers offer all sorts of free events that are usually just upsells into more expensive programs or ill-fitting property solutions.

So, they may end up 'saving pennies but paying pounds'.

The 'I'll try everything at the buffet' investor

Of course, not everyone wants to short-change their education. Some people understand the value of a good education and are happy to pay for it. These investors are not to be confused with Warren Buffett – the 'I'll try everything at the buffet' investor wants to taste it all.

> 'Few things are brought to a successful issue by impetuous desire, but most by calm and prudent forethought.'
>
> *Thucydides*

In fact, some people have gone out and bought everything they can – books, DVDs, tickets to events, courses – and have paid for some very expensive coaching (my eyes water at what some people are charging in this space). They have some impressive libraries to show for it – many of which are simply collecting dust.

Unfortunately, usually their property investing results are not as impressive as their libraries because they have spent a large chunk of their available capital on courses and 'VIP weekend retreats', leaving little money left to actually invest. These investors are always on the hunt for that one course or program that will give them the magic recipe for building wealth without having to put in the real effort and time required to successfully achieve their financial goals.

The impatient investor

Not someone to be bothered with such trivial matters as getting a good education or developing a clear plan, the impatient investor has money to spend and, damn it, they are going to spend it come hell or high water. The impatient investor is not scared of throwing their money into the markets to see what happens. I have a name for that: I call it gambling!

Impatient investors are only too happy to bypass all that boring learning stuff to get rich. And why not? They are hopefully young enough, lucky enough and have enough money to burn to be able to absorb any setbacks along the way.

The upfront education costs may seem low to the impatient investor, but the true cost of this type of 'coalface' education may not be known for many years to come.

> 'The two most powerful warriors are patience and time.'
>
> Leo Tolstoy

Let's use a commonly told joke to illustrate another point that is often overlooked by the impatient investor.

An old bull and a young bull are walking through the fields when they come to the top of a rise. Down below they see a whole herd of cows. The young bull gets all excited and turns to the old bull and says, 'Let's run down the hill and make passionate love to one of those cows', to which the older bull says, 'No... let's walk down the hill and make passionate love to them all!'

Okay, when I first heard this joke it was a slightly less G-rated version than I have told here, but the message in it for all property investors still holds true. Sometimes we are too quick to charge after a goal, not realising that a far bigger prize is there for the taking if only we take a different approach. And that all comes down to your plan, which I discuss in depth in chapter 14.

The burnt or 'heavily singed' investor

As the name implies, the burnt investor is someone who has lost money investing in the past. This type of investor may have had a bad experience buying olive trees, lost money in superannuation during the global financial crisis (GFC), bought a dud investment property or had a bad experience in the share market.

It is often the case that the investor has 'spent money' on something but has not truly 'invested' because they never really understood what they were investing in. Most likely, they only lost money because they didn't invest enough time upfront in their education and planning before forking out their cash.

To rub salt into the wound, they may have purchased a dud property and then sold it just before the market recovered, crystallising their losses. No doubt they are still complaining about that 'bit of bad luck' too.

> 'If at first you don't succeed… so much for skydiving.'
>
> Henny Youngman

Basically, burnt investors have made some mistakes in the past and have never gotten over it. Their inability to let go of the past, learn from their mistakes and create a better strategy has held them back ever since. Sadly, they haven't owned the outcome of their investing, taken responsibility for it, and so they look outwards for someone or something to blame forever and a day.

You hear the burnt investor saying, 'Don't invest in property, I tried it once and it didn't work!'

The cynical investor

I am all for a dose of healthy scepticism when questions or doubts are accompanied by a genuinely curious and open mind. Challenging the status quo, pushing boundaries and not accepting mediocrity is, after all, something I pride myself on.

However, closed-minded cynicism is not healthy. Many people get so caught up trying to find ways to prove how right they are that they are never truly effective. In our opinion, you'll rarely find a wealthy cynic.

Cynics can, however, be a lot of fun to work with. They usually think that everything is a scam and that everyone is out to rip them off. These investors are often a combination of burnt and wannabe investors. They may be new to investing but they have heard all the horror stories, and often they have little education or no background in investing – or they have largely experienced negative outcomes. The cynical investor often becomes sceptical after hearing about the negative experiences of their friends or family. They haven't necessarily had a bad personal experience themselves, but they have read the papers, so they know what's going on!

Of course, this has nothing to do with them and everything to do with the fact that the world is full of snake-oil salesmen and conspiracy theorists.

They are cynical of every investment strategy and everyone they encounter who discusses their finances in any way, shape or form.

> 'What is a cynic? Someone who knows the price of everything and the value of nothing.'
>
> Oscar Wilde

While it's normal to be sceptical, and I always encourage people to ask good questions, these investors can't trust themselves to be able to make the right decisions and therefore, by extension, can't trust anyone else to help them either.

The problem with cynical investors is that they get in their own way. The first step these investors have to take to get better results is to come to the conclusion that the strategy they are using to get ahead simply isn't working for them. If they spent more time educating themselves on what could work, rather than focusing on what doesn't, then maybe they could improve their results.

The been-there-done-that investor

The been-there-done-that investor will start conversations with, 'Okay, so show me what you've got'. Having passed the early barriers to investing, they know that the right type of investment can make them a profit. Investors who have enjoyed some degree of success in the past may erroneously think that they know it all.

They may say they are open to looking at new opportunities, but often they just want to continue in the same way all by themselves. As they have had 'successes' in the past, regardless of how big or small they have been, their egos get in the way and they are too proud to ask for help, even if it could take them to the next level safer, faster or more predictably. Yet they are still out there looking for more information on investing because deep down they know there is probably a better way.

> 'By three methods we may learn wisdom:
> First, by reflection, which is noblest; Second,
> by imitation, which is easiest; and third by
> experience, which is the bitterest.'
>
> *Confucius*

Another name for this guy is the know-it-all investor! They typically follow a very ad-hoc approach to investing. They jump from strategy to strategy because they have never taken the time to develop any form of clear plan. But that's okay, because they will be the first to tell you that they know what they are doing!

The aha! investor

The aha! investor has broken through many of the barriers that the other seven investor types mentioned haven't. They understand that all investment carries some level of risk, but they also understand that they need to take action for anything to change. It is up to them to change their financial future – they are the only one responsible for their decisions.

> 'Genius is one per cent inspiration and
> ninety-nine per cent perspiration.'
>
> *Thomas A. Edison*

The aha! investor has let go of their ego, decided to ask for help and is building an expert team. They accept that they don't know everything and are willing to get their hands dirty if necessary, but also know when it is better to delegate certain tasks to the professionals. Beyond making that shift, they accept that they will need to educate themselves, create a clear plan, surround themselves with great people and know that achieving the results they want is going to take time.

The armchair investor

The armchair investor is typically a high-income earner who believes in the concept of outsourcing and has a trusted team of advisers to help them. They understand that their skillset is typically best focused on their line of work or passions, and that to build wealth they are better off having a team of people to work in their chosen investment field, do the time-consuming research and due diligence and share it with them.

This type of investor sees value in having a mentor to assist them on their journey. They know that they cannot do everything themselves and can often get a better result by getting external help. They are focused on value, not cost, because they know the difference between the two. They also know that, especially in the service industry, you get what you pay for much of the time.

*

I acknowledge that there are numerous variations on the investor types discussed in this chapter. But there are only two groups that can succeed at a high level – the aha! investor and the armchair investor. If you fit into any of the other types, that's okay, because that means there is room to grow, and with growth comes new experiences, and that allows you to change!

Chapter 6

All investors have something to fear

'Fears are educated into us and can, if we wish, be educated out.'

Karl Augustus Menninger

Does each of the investor types profiled in the previous chapter have the potential to grow a massive property portfolio? Yes, absolutely! All of these investors have some things in common:

- They all like the idea of investing and, most likely, all want to build wealth through property to achieve their goals.
- They do not have a specific plan of exactly how they are going to achieve their goals or by when.
- The one thing that adversely affects most of them is *fear*.

Investor fears

I am yet to meet an investor who does not fear something. The first step for all investors, therefore, is to work out what that 'something' is and tackle it head on.

#LetsGetReal
All investors fear something. It's how they handle their fear that sets them apart.

Fear of losing money

The wannabe investor fears losing what little money they have and therefore would prefer to research and research until the cows come home. Protecting and preserving their small amount of capital is a fear-driven emotional phenomenon.

Simply hoping that somehow their investment capital will magically multiply in their sleep is unlikely to bring much success. They also hang their hat on every piece of negative news that comes out of the media as proof to their family and friends that they were right to be cautious. These guys and gals probably also buy lotto tickets – but don't get me started on that 'strategy'!

The fear surrounding the wannabe investor often comes down to a lack of investment experience, and they are mostly motivated by the fear of losing money!

Fear of not having enough to invest

The frugal investor often fears that, by spending money on their education, they will have less money to spend on their investing. Or, they fear that they will spend money on their education and be unable to get a return on that investment because they can't back themselves to be able to apply anything they learn successfully (no matter how small that initial investment is!).

Fear of missing out

The I'll-try-everything-at-the-buffet investor and the impatient investor fear missing out. You hear these types of investors saying, 'What if I don't buy this and I miss out on the one special piece of knowledge that is going to turn all of my results around?' or,

'If I don't get into the market straight away, prices will go up and I will miss out'. Sound familiar?

Property spruikers love these guys and gals – they are their preferred prey. They lure their victims in with claims such as 'Quick! If you race to the back of the room now and sign up for this course/event/property, for today only you will pay only $X instead of the usual $X + $10,000. That's a saving of $10,000 – but it's for today only'.

Most likely, whatever they are flogging is way overpriced, and it will be that same price again tomorrow, at the exact same event in the next city along, with the next group of suckers.

Unfortunately, these sales tactics still seem to work today. I wish they had been left back in the 1980s and 1990s where they came from; hopefully future investors will start waking up to these slimy tactics. It churns my stomach to hear from good people who have been conned by these slick salespeople. In today's world, with social media ubiquitous and our digital footprints expanding, I am starting to see the bad eggs exposed – like cockroaches scurrying when the lights are suddenly turned on.

Sadly, though, some of these spruikers couldn't care less about being in the spotlight; these are the cowboys I mentioned earlier. They know that there is always someone out there who will fall for their latest scheme regardless of the negative press or online social media commentary. Again, like the cockroach, they never seem to die – they keep crawling back!

Fear that history may repeat itself

The fears of the burnt investor stem from their previous bad experiences and that history may repeat itself. Of course, most often it was probably their lack of education, lack of a plan and lack of the right professional support structures that caused their previous poor results.

However, because none of that has changed, their fear of having the same thing happen again quite literally stops them in their tracks. Some people have lost everything – the family home, their business or job – and countless marriages have ended due to poor investment decisions and lack of planning.

Overcoming this fear can be difficult, but it is absolutely necessary to get to the next level.

Fear of looking stupid

The cynical investor's fears are an exaggerated version of the wannabe investor's. They have heard the bad stories and, while they might know that there are countless opportunities to create wealth, they are scared of repeating the mistakes of their family or friends and looking just plain dumb.

'Who would want to be in the newspapers like those suckers who lost money? Not me!' They are so scared of being ripped off or losing their hard-earned money that they often do nothing.

Fear of asking for help

The been-there-done-that investor's fears are about letting go and asking for help. They fear that this may make them look weak or inexperienced. Unfortunately, their pride will often stop them from building on their earlier successes and taking their results to the next level.

They would hate to think that there is possibly a better way or that they may have been wrong. The fear of having their pride hurt, or reputation tarnished, is usually subconsciously stopping them from getting ahead.

Fear of everything but overcoming that fear

Even the aha! investor has fears. They have fears about making wrong decisions just like anyone else. They have fears around choosing the wrong team to support them and they have fears about losing money or choosing the wrong investment strategy. The difference is that they don't fear finding ways to overcome this fear and they don't let their fears stop them from moving forward.

Handling your fear

The first step in handling your fear is to identify that there is a problem and then, of course, admit it. The next is to find out how you actually go about fixing things.

It comes down to doing a few key things:

1. You have to deal with any emotional blockages you may have and be emotionally ready to start investing in a way that will achieve results (refer back to chapter 3).
2. You need to understand WHY you are investing. Then you can start to create a real strategic plan for how you are going to invest.
3. Most investors are actually suffering from information overwhelm, not insufficient information. There is a missing link between information and results.
4. Even investors who have done their homework may still lack the confidence to get started. Remember, a lack of confidence will usually stem from not completing steps 1 and 2 here. Without a clear understanding of what your personal wealth strategy is, based around your own unique risk–reward profiling, then all the information in the world is just that.

#LetsGetReal
The whole purpose of getting properly educated is to bridge the gap between information and results.

> **Mentor tip**
> In my experience, working one-on-one with one of The Property Mentors' experienced mentors over time is often the safest, fastest and most reliable way to bridge that gap.

Let's take a look at a case study.

Case study: Barry and Jane become property investors

The media publish some amazing articles about how well the property market is performing and so Jane says to Barry, 'Hey babe, I think we should get ourselves an investment property. Tiffany, the receptionist from the office, just bought an investment property, so why shouldn't we be looking into it?'

'Sure', says Barry. 'One of my mates from work is looking at some properties too'.

So, the happy couple head out on the weekend to look at properties. They go out armed with their iPad and the local newspaper with some property listings in their area circled (yes, people still do that). They have saved a list of properties that they intend to look at and they make a few calls to agents in the area. Given that they have already bought their own home in the area a few years ago, they know it's a nice place to live, and so of course it's a great area to invest. Why wouldn't tenants want to live there? They love it!

Barry and Jane begin their walk through the first property that is open for inspection. The agent does the typical 'meet and greet' and asks them what they are looking for. The couple are still quite new at this, so they brush off the agent and look around the property. At this point they are 'just looking'. After all, they are investors now and they are just doing their 'research'.

After looking at a few properties, they pluck up the courage to ask a few questions of one of the agents they have met that day who they seem to get along with. They ask intelligent questions such as 'How long has this property been on the market?' and 'Is the price negotiable?'

The real estate agent saw them coming a mile away. He answers their questions and praises them for asking such intelligent questions. Then the big question is asked: 'Would this make a good investment property?'

'Since you know the area, you will appreciate that this property would make a great investment', is the agent's reply. 'It has a nice garden and presents well – it would be *ideal* for tenants.'

The real estate agent has no idea whether it will make a good investment or not. Many real estate agents do not even own investment properties themselves. The agent has done the right thing by the vendor and built rapport with the happy couple in an effort to sell the property.

Barry and Jane are now convinced that, because they know the area and the media is reporting positive news on the overall property market, they may just miss out if they don't get in now.

Of course, the agent has told them that someone else is going through the property tomorrow morning for a second look and they are interested in putting in an offer. (Ever heard that one before?) The happy couple have now spent a few weekends looking at properties, so they think they have a pretty good feel for the market.

The agent suggests that other properties in the area (not as good as this one) have sold really quickly and so, with the excitement of becoming property investors and the thought of becoming rich, they decide to put in an offer. The problem is that Barry and Jane actually think the agent is on their side the whole time.

There are many problems with this scenario.

> **#LetsGetReal**
> The real estate agent is acting for the vendor and *not* for the buyer. In fact, he has a fiduciary duty to put the vendor's interests first at all times.

Where did they go wrong?

Barry and Jane's experience highlights a common flaw in most property investors' thinking: they think that investing starts and ends with the property itself. If you are reading this book, you should be realising that there is a great deal more to investing than finding a property.

But you can't build a property portfolio without property, right?

True. But these guys have simply bought a property for investment, and the textbook definition is that they have become property investors. However, without a clear plan and direction they are most likely not going to become successful property investors long term. They may get some results, but all too often investors like our lovely couple here never get the sustainable 'cash cow' property portfolio they thought they would end up with. Unless you treat your property investing like a business, chances are you may only ever get the results of someone investing as a hobby.

I've heard every excuse in the book

Over the last few years, I've spoken with thousands of people who are currently investing or want to invest in property – believe me when I say I have literally heard it *all*. I have heard the good, the bad, the ugly and the downright messy.

Last year, a gentleman from Queensland told me that he would not invest in Victoria 'because he lost money on a property there once'. When I challenged him on this and said, 'So, what you are saying is that you are ruling out investing in Victoria because you made a bad decision once?' the phone went silent.

I asked him another question: 'Do you think there are people who are making money investing in property in Victoria?' After another pause he responded with, 'Of course'.

'So, why can't you?' I asked.

He responded, 'I don't know enough about it'.

Well, there you go!

People will always make up excuses and little dramas in their own heads to convince themselves why they should, or shouldn't, do something.

#LetsGetReal
Take a minute to reflect. What ideas do you have in your head that could be stopping you? Think about it. What is that really? It's called fear.

This may come as a shock to many, but it will be exceedingly difficult or take an incredibly long time to become financially independent with just one or two average-priced properties purchased in an average way. So, if you have a couple of investment properties right now, chances are you are going to need to keep working at building that portfolio if your goal is to be financially free from your property portfolio alone in a reasonable timeframe.

If you are yet to get started, that's probably a good thing because you have the benefit of reading this book first, which will help you begin that journey correctly and ensure that first step you take is in the right direction.

In the next chapter I take a look at the difference between investors and speculators. Why do you need to know this? Read on and it will become clear.

Chapter 7

Speculating vs investing

'Our plans miscarry because they have no aim.
When you don't know what harbour you're
aiming for, no wind is the right wind.'

Lucius Annaeus Seneca

It is probably prudent that we all agree now, before we get too far into this, just exactly what differentiates investing from speculating.

In the case study in the previous chapter, Barry and Jane did what a lot of people do – they went out there into the marketplace and started looking at property. Once they found a property they liked, they went and bought it. The biggest problem with this is that they had no plan and no strategy behind the purchase. They didn't really know why they bought the property.

Barry and Jane technically bought an investment property. But, in my view, they were speculating, not investing.

I consider that you are investing if you:

1. follow a plan
2. know your return on investment (ROI)
3. have a timeframe to achieve your ROI for that investment
4. know your level of risk.

Ideally, you should be fairly confident that you have this knowledge *before* you part with your hard-earned money.

In property, some things cannot be known. Markets can change, and property prices can go up or down as well as stay the same for long periods of time. But the key to successful investing is having as much of your outcome known in advance as possible. Then you are truly investing.

As Barry and Jane were not following any sort of investment plan, they did not know if they'd even bought at fair market value, let alone what that property might be worth in the future.

As a professional property investor, I take a more commercial approach to my investing. All decisions are treated as business decisions and are made as part of an investment plan that focuses on achieving specific goals.

#LetsGetReal
Every property I acquire, every investment I make, every development I do has a *specific purpose*, and that doesn't happen by accident.

I started out like the majority of investors by just going out there and buying properties and trying every property strategy under the sun – with no plan of attack. So, I certainly can't blame you for doing the same thing, and I am not judging you for it. There is currently little genuine guidance and advice out there that you can depend on in the long term.

Mentor tip
Our main driving force at The Property Mentors is to provide genuine resources and education to investors and to see them use these tools to succeed.

Working towards your goals

If you think about the reasons you are investing in the first place, ultimately it's because you have goals that you wish to achieve. Simple!

Imagine everything you want to accomplish in life is like a finished jigsaw puzzle. You start to achieve your goal of finishing the puzzle one piece at a time, adding to the puzzle over time. Similarly, think of each property in your portfolio as one piece of that jigsaw puzzle. Depending on the size of your goals and the total value of properties you are aiming for in your portfolio, you may only have a few pieces in your jigsaw puzzle or you may need dozens and dozens of pieces to achieve your end goal.

Either way, you need to start with the end in mind. This means basically looking at the box and seeing the completed picture before you even touch the very first piece of the puzzle. As investors, you don't rush out and buy a piece of the jigsaw puzzle without knowing how it fits into the big picture and whether it is even the right piece in the first place.

> **#LetsGetReal**
> Property investors who buy property without knowing what their jigsaw puzzle looks like are setting themselves up to fail. I can't stress this enough because I have seen it time and time again.

Can you imagine even trying to complete a jigsaw puzzle without the picture on the box to guide you?

If you want to 'dabble' in property, that's great and I wish you well. I know first-hand the power of building wealth through property, but we are talking about long-term, sustainable property portfolios that can provide security and income for the rest of your life. That is a big deal and I take it very seriously.

I teach people that investing in property is a long-term gig, not something designed to help you make a quick buck. As you probably know, there are countless get-rich-quick opportunities out there promising the world, packaged up to sound too good to be true. As I've said earlier, the reason these types of businesses pop up time and time again is that suckers still fall for their tricks. The sharks and cowboys of the property industry are not there to help you for the long term. They have no vested interest in your success and usually only have one outcome that they care about – getting a sale! It's completely transactional.

Sure, there are deals out there where you may be able to make a quick buck, and you may get lucky once or twice, but the problem is that chasing the fastest dollar is often a footrace you will lose.

Additionally, this approach is rarely sustainable and is difficult to replicate. It is a bit like trying to catch lightning in a bottle: it's hard to do and more than a little bit dangerous!

Investing sustainably can be – and I would argue it probably should be – a little bit boring. But boring doesn't sell! So, the wealth creation and property investment industry has come up with a whole bunch of what I like to refer to as 'shiny objects' – those cool-sounding things that distract you from the fundamentals and your plans and goals.

Returning to the jigsaw analogy, a get-rich-quick opportunity is like finding a piece of the jigsaw that simply doesn't connect with any of the other bits. You can try to fit it in but, even if it joins up with one other piece, it just won't fit into the bigger picture.

The only reason spruikers keep popping up is, purely and simply, greed. Greed drives these unscrupulous operators to put profits before people. And it is the same greed that attracts investors wanting mega profits in short timeframes.

> **Mentor tip**
> By getting distracted by shiny objects, you risk making a bad investment, losing your capital and having to start all over. It happens every day of the week.

Taking all this into consideration, I hear you ask, 'How do I get a plan and where can I find my own jigsaw puzzle box to follow?'

How can you safely navigate your way through the minefields to make sure your investing strategy uses all the right bits of the jigsaw puzzle? Keep reading.

> **Mentor tip**
> You are going to pay for your education one way or another. It is better to invest your money in yourself before investing it in anything you don't understand.

Chapter 8

Out of the hot tub and into a bigger and better one!

'Progress is impossible without change, and those who cannot change their minds cannot change anything.'

George Bernard Shaw

May I ask you a favour? Is it okay if I bypass all the superficial stuff? May I please skip the normal pleasantries and choose not to talk about the weather or what you did on the weekend or which school your kids go to? Because, to be frank, I don't see how any of that will help you fast-track your investment strategy!

Operating at the surface might make us all feel okay, but it will not get us where we need to be – not if we want to fast-track our results and not if we really want to get real. If all we do is scratch the surface, it will simply not allow us to have the level of conversation that is required to be able to transform your life.

The sort of places we need to go to get real results can be frightening for some people. The level of emotional honesty I insist upon in my mentoring can be alarming and can end our journey before we even get going, because it all gets too real too soon. For others, this is just the tonic they have been searching for.

If there is a series of goals that you want to achieve, changing your behaviour and overcoming negative habits can be challenging. It's often hard. If it wasn't, everyone would already have everything they want in life.

Life does not usually reward those who only take the easy path – especially at the start. As with a lot of things in life, it usually gets easier the further along you go. I think this thing called life has been deliberately designed to be hard at the start to weed out those who are *simply curious* from those who are *truly serious* about living a life full of wealth and abundance. If you can accept and embrace that, then make the decision to go out and change your life anyway – you will be surprised by the doors that open for you.

Are you ready?

> 'Waking up to who you are requires letting go of who you imagine yourself to be.'
>
> *Alan Watts*

Are you ready to make the decision to get real and step up? Ready to raise the standards of what you will tolerate in your life and challenge yourself to discover what you are truly capable of? Because if you can get real with yourself, face your fears, continue to push yourself and continue to be open to learning and growing as a human being, something remarkable can happen. Your life can change in ways you never even imagined possible.

If you are not ready now, let me ask you, 'How much time do you have left to make these changes?' If you are not ready now, when will you be ready? 'Someday' is not a day of the week, and it is unlikely that your life is going to become magically less busy, less stressful or more enjoyable without making the decision to make those results a reality.

You've got to learn to tune out the critics – often the harshest critic is within you – and get to work on your goals and your life. Most people will spend more time planning an overseas holiday for just a couple of weeks than they will spend planning out a whole lifetime of joy, happiness and wonder. Let's face it, planning a holiday is easy, but planning a truly remarkable life – now, that takes work, commitment and a lot of courage.

> **Mentor tip**
> If you don't make plans for your ideal life, nobody is going to do it for you!

You see, in life, most of us have drifted away from our real truth and have landed on an alternate version of reality. We have built up personas or avatars, if you like, for how we see ourselves in the world, or how we would want others to view us.

I recently heard a sad tale about an otherwise normal 70-year-old divorcee who found himself lost for years playing *World of Warcraft* to the extent that he lost tens of thousands of real dollars when online hackers stole his online armour and left him without protection in the game. The gap between perceived reality and the truth got even worse for him when he fell in love with a 'lady' playing the game online. Their online relationship blossomed and he even started paying for her life outside the game – she happily accepted his gifts and payments. It wasn't until he wanted to bring the relationship from online to offline that he realised he was the victim of a dating scam.

This is by no means an isolated incident. This phenomenon has been termed 'catfishing' and there is a whole TV series about the people this happens to. No doubt you have better things to do with your time than watch it, however.

To some extent, we have all built up avatars for how we want to be perceived in the world and we have accumulated emotional armour throughout the course of our lives. So, despite the fact that it may feel as if these personas we have built up are real, the truth is often they are just façades designed to protect us emotionally.

Leaving your comfort zone

> 'The best things in life are often waiting for you at the exit ramp of your comfort zone.'
>
> Karen Salmansohn

As you progress through this book, like a turtle without a shell, you are going to feel uncomfortable, vulnerable and exposed if you decide to remove any of this armour.

But, in life, that is where growth occurs – in discomfort, not comfort!

For most of us, life is too comfortable. Imagine your life as like sitting in a hot tub right now. If the water is hot enough and the jets are strong enough, you have no reason to want to ever get out.

Now imagine that the hot water is suddenly replaced by buckets of ice-cold freezing water.

You will most likely jump out of that tub faster than a cat on a hot tin roof (or faster than Australia rolls its prime ministers!). You see, human beings are largely driven by two emotional states – pain or pleasure (unlike cats, who are simply creatures of pleasure and leisure, as anyone who has owned a cat will tell you).

> **Mentor tip**
>
> In my experience, pain is out in front of pleasure by a country mile when it comes to motivating change in people's lives.

The only two things that will get you out of your own hot tub of life are either a painful event (like the cold water) or a strong pull towards a more pleasurable event somewhere else. For most people, until the temperature gets too cold (or too hot), or the jets stop working, they will just continue to drift along in their own little hot tub of life – relaxed, comfortable and content.

How much pain will it take to get you moving?

If you currently rely on having to turn up somewhere to work to generate the income you need to run your lifestyle, let's look at this another way. Right now, you have a comfort range for the level of income your lifestyle can handle.

If, for example, you are earning near the Australian average full-time wage of around $94,000 per annum, you could maybe handle that income dropping to $80,000 without too much pain in your life. You would maybe make a few minor adjustments to your lifestyle, such as eating out less often, and simply adapt and carry on. Using the hot tub of life analogy, the water has only cooled slightly, not enough to make you want to get out – and certainly not in a hurry.

But if your annual income dropped to $60,000 or $40,000 or, worse still, you lost your job altogether, then all of a sudden you would be having to make some pretty big changes to your lifestyle. In other words, that hot tub of yours is no longer so hot and you are going to have to get out of your comfort zone until you can find a new way to become comfortable again.

Most of us don't want to experience pain or discomfort regularly. The underlying motivation in most people's lives is 'How do I do just enough to avoid pain so I am not required to change anything in my life?'

Far fewer people ask the better question, 'How can I experience more ___ in my life?' (for example, more love, wealth, happiness, satisfaction, pride… well, you get the idea).

Challenge yourself

> 'Everything you want is just outside your comfort zone.'
> Robert Allen

Your comfort zone is a nice, cosy place – it's comfortable. Successful people, no matter what their profession or skillset, operate mostly from outside their comfort zones and seek to constantly expand what they find comfortable.

> **#LetsGetReal**
> Successful people deliberately challenge themselves to grow. They are at the top of their games because they push the boundaries, and they are at their most excited when they are uncomfortable. They often enjoy the process of growing and stepping outside their comfort zones.

Most people don't want to leave their comfort zone. In fact, the whole human nervous system is designed to stop us from experiencing pain. We are hardwired to want to avoid pain at all costs.

So, how do we do it? How do we push past those natural tendencies to stay safe and comfortable? And how is getting out of our comfort zones even going to help us build wealth through property?

Mentor tip
Make getting out of your comfort zone a way of life, not just a once-off challenge.

I am not for one moment saying that this is going to be easy. When you are in your comfort zone, you already know what to expect.

People often stick to what is familiar to them when it comes to property investing.

For example, a property investor from Western Australia may have a few properties in Perth but wouldn't consider investing on the east coast of Australia because they fear that they don't understand the markets there. So, instead of challenging themselves to learn and move out of their comfort zone, they may only keep buying property in Perth because it feels 'safe'.

Equally, other investors only buy growth-zone house-and-land and wouldn't consider investing in inner-city apartments. When you are inside a comfort zone, life is easier – you know the boundaries and it feels 'safe'.

They say ignorance is bliss… but what if it is just ignorance?

Sure, staying inside your comfort zone may be easier, but where is the fun and excitement in that? It is only when you step outside your comfort zone that the magic happens. That's where you grow, and once you grow it's hard to ever return to the way you were.

I challenge you to consider what comfort zones you are currently experiencing and what is stopping you from expanding your comfort levels.

> **#LetsGetReal**
> Unfortunately, 'close enough' or 'this will have to do' are common catchphrases for many a frustrated investor. It is important to highlight that in life you don't always get what you want, but you will always get what you tolerate.

What are you guilty of merely tolerating? Consider this by asking yourself the following questions:

- Have you given up on any of the dreams, desires and goals you once had for yourself?
- Has your fear of losing what you currently have stopped you from asking for more from your life?
- Have you simply settled for what you already have?

If these questions make you feel uncomfortable, that's good – they are designed to! The answers to these questions most likely haven't been the result of conscious actions – things have simply happened during your life that have distracted you from your financial goals and ambitions.

As you have given me permission to mentor you through this process, I have to shake the trees to see what is going to fall out. Don't worry, I will catch everything that falls, and if you want you can stick it all back up there in the tree again if you choose to later.

No doubt you have picked up this book because you have a desire to get better results from your investing and your life. In your mind right now, there is something that you perceive you lack to fulfill that mission. If there wasn't, you would be out there getting on with the job, right?

So, let me ask you:

'What is it that you think you don't have enough of?'

Write it down:

My life would be so much better if only I had _____

Or:

If only I knew _____

Or:

If I were better at _____

What is the magic ingredient (or ingredients) missing for you to fulfill your destiny?

These are challenging questions. Even if you could answer them right now, chances are the answers you give won't solve the actual problems you need to solve.

Let's finish this chapter with an example of a conversation I had with a mentee to highlight what I mean. (I have changed the person's name in this case study to protect their privacy.)

Case study: Joe's investing journey

Joe is 64 years old and has been working for almost 46 years – he still works to this day. He has been investing in property for 28 years and is always chasing the highest returns. If he loses every now and then, he will make it up on another investment. In his words, 'If I have my finger in many pies, I am reducing my chance of anything going wrong'.

Joe continues to make sacrifices and lives a modest lifestyle so he can keep investing. When I challenged him as to why he was investing in the first place and why he still gets up each day to go to a full-time job, he was quite disturbed by the question. His approach had worked for him, to some extent, and he simply wanted to discuss other high-yielding investment options with me.

I told him that my approach is to discuss the reasons WHY he is investing first rather than rush into discussing a particular investment, as that would be doing him a disservice. When we stepped back and had a conversation about the real reasons why he was investing, it came down (in order of his priorities) to:

1. leaving a legacy for his children and grandchildren
2. providing for himself and his wife into retirement
3. enjoying the thrill of investing and the process of making money.

I challenged him on his number-one goal, to leave a legacy for his children and grandchildren, by asking him what that looked like to him. He responded by saying, 'When I die, I want to leave my kids with money so that they can live a good life'.

I responded with, 'You have enough money to live a comfortable retirement now. Do you think your kids want you to keep scrimping, sacrificing and working in a job you don't particularly enjoy just to give them money when you die?'

'I had never thought about it like that', he said.

Then I asked him, 'Do you think that if you stopped working your full-time job, you would have enough money to retire now, provide for yourself and your wife for the years ahead and still be able to leave money for your family?'

'Absolutely', he said.

'So, what is stopping you? Do you think that, if you shifted your focus away from leaving a financial windfall behind and focused on spending more time with your family now and teaching them what you have learned over the last 28 years, they would be happier? They would not only enjoy spending time with you, but you will have the opportunity to educate them on how you have built your investment portfolio. And, in the end, if you are still able to leave them some money, your legacy will live on much longer than the money you leave them.'

Joe's response was the lightbulb moment I often hear that makes my hard work worth it.

'From the bottom of my heart, thank you. Nobody has ever had a conversation like that with me in all my years as an investor. You are completely right.'

Joe discovered through this process that what he really wanted was to leave his family with great experiences and memories – not just cold hard cash. Joe admitted that he has only been investing in high-risk investments as he gets older because he was so focused on leaving each family member a certain dollar figure and he hadn't achieved that to date. He was instead risking missing that goal simply because in his mind he was running out of time.

To get that desired result, Joe was willing to work until he turned 70 years old and keep investing in these high-risk investments. However, when we drilled down, he realised that he was missing out on spending time with his family and teaching them what he had learned. This ended up being more important to him once we defined what his legacy actually meant to him.

Joe's focus now is to invest his funds in opportunities that are safer and lower-risk and to retire within 12 months to spend more time with his family and grandchildren. This was a wake-up call for Joe that made him realise what was truly important in his life.

Lastly, Joe admitted that his frugality was making his wife upset. They had enough money to live a great life in retirement, but for the last few years he had neglected to take her out for dinner, travel and enjoy their life together. Joe is now investing more in enjoying time with his wife and appreciating the wealth he has already accumulated.

Did I tell Joe what to do? Nope. Did I ask him some really powerful questions so that he could come up with the answers himself? Absolutely.

Mentor tip
Just because you are on a certain pathway doesn't mean that you need to stay on it if you discover it is the wrong one.

Chapter 9

Are we there yet?

*'The universe is change;
our life is what our thoughts make it.'*

Marcus Aurelius

Have you ever heard the saying, 'We are living in an ever-changing world'? Well, duh! When was the world ever the same from one year to the next? Of course it's ever-changing.

But that is not a valid excuse for people to avoid making important decisions about their own futures or to create a plan for their life.

Some people erroneously think that, just because the world is changing, it is best not to make any plans because they are likely to have to be changed anyway. They might say to themselves, 'Let's just keep doing what we have been doing, at least until we know what will happen after whatever changes ahead have already happened'!

Have a think about that for a moment. Examine the thought process behind this idea and think about the excuses.

Let's break it down even further. To illustrate the point, here are some excuses (and the reasoning behind them) that I often hear.

EXCUSE #1

Thought process: I can't predict what is going to happen in the future, so how can I plan for it?

Fear: What if I spend my valuable time planning out a better life but then have to change those plans?

Truth: You will most likely have to adjust and change your plans over time – sometimes because of external events and sometimes because you, and what is most important to you, will change during the journey.

EXCUSE #2

Thought process: My plans may not work out exactly as I want them to.

Fear: If I don't achieve my goals then I may look like a failure.

Truth: Being held accountable to the things you want to achieve in life can be intimidating for some people. But, in reality, wouldn't you prefer to aim for something better in life and just miss it, rather than not aim for anything much at all and hit it?

Remember in chapter 4 when I asked you to consider how serious you were about building wealth? I asked if you were just looking to 'give it a go' or if you were 100% committed to the process. What I am getting at is that, whatever your reason for picking up this book, there is a good chance you are looking to improve your life in some way – even if you are still only curious and not yet fully serious about the process.

Consider these questions

Let's pause for a moment and consider a few more serious questions.

What percentage of your life do you think you have significant control over, and how much of your life have you just let happen to you?

Write down your answers in the spaces below:

In control _____ % vs Out of control _____ %

Now, have a think about how you have been doing things to this point in your life and ask yourself:

- What have you been doing for the past 5, 10, 15 or more years?
- What has worked for you and what hasn't?
- How and where have you invested your time?

As you've picked up this book, you are most likely looking to build and grow a solid and secure property portfolio. But it's likely that you are going to need to do some things differently to what you have been doing to achieve these goals.

Can we all agree on that? Yes?

In the previous chapter, I explained that doing anything new is usually going to feel uncomfortable before it feels comfortable. In addition, doing something new is scary for a lot of people. That is perfectly normal.

Now for a couple more questions:

- Are you going to let what scares you stop you from achieving your goals in life?
- Are you willing to get out of your comfort zone, learn new things, work with different people and invest differently to how you have in the past?

Let's explore this further with an example that most people will be able to relate to.

Why are some people simply more successful than others?

> 'Knowing is not enough; we must apply.
> Willing is not enough; we must do.'
>
> Johann Wolfgang von Goethe

Think about this (and yes, I will continue to challenge you to do lots of self-reflection). In your current line of work, are there people who are *more* successful than you are in your job or business?

Now, unless you are the equivalent of Bill Gates or Oprah Winfrey in your industry then the answer is probably going to be yes!

Next, consider whether, in your line of work, there are people who are *less* successful than you are? No doubt!

That's interesting, isn't it? But, to be clear, it doesn't mean that you are a better or worse person than anyone else, simply that the other person has been able to become more or less successful than you in your chosen career or business.

For example, for every decent plumber there is a plumber who is even more successful and better at what they do. Equally, there are plenty of plumbers who are not as good and nowhere near as successful in their work. But, if we think about it, in order to become plumbers all of these people had to go through similar training. They all went to trade school, completed assessments or exams and did an apprenticeship for four years or more. So, they all had access to pretty much the same information and training. Why, then, are some people simply more successful than others?

Coming back to you, would it be fair to say that you may have done some things differently to the less-successful person in your line of work? Maybe you attended a few more trade events or seminars, did more study in your own time or had a stronger *commitment* to become better.

The same goes for the people who are more successful than you. They probably did some of the same things as you, but they took it to another level. They did even *more* work to succeed, read more books, studied more and took massive action to grow their knowledge and skills to get to where they wanted to be. As I cover in chapter 15, these people probably started out with the end in mind and had a specific goal to achieve that result – it didn't happen by chance.

Emotional attachment

In any field, it is often the emotional attachment to the end result that will largely determine your success. Sure, talent, dedication, desire, commitment (and good looks) are important, but they are the result of the emotional connection or passion that you have attached to the outcome.

It is this emotional connection that most investors need help with in the first instance and the reason I have written this book. In fact, I estimate that at least 80% of your investment success will come down to your ability to manage your emotions.

It's especially difficult for us men, who generally don't want to talk about our emotions. We are happy to talk about the footy, or what we got up to over the weekend, but connecting at a deep level with our feelings and what we want to achieve in our lifetimes… that's not (generally speaking) what we're used to.

The other 20% of investment success will come down to specific knowledge and skillsets – the logical and transactional side of investing. This is where your specific industry knowledge, networks and access to your A-Team will come into play. (More about this side of investing in chapter 18.)

> **#LetsGetReal**
> It took a lot of introspection, and many uncomfortable moments, before I was able to talk about this sort of stuff. As hard as it is to admit and to believe, I am not perfect. We can all improve in one area of our lives or another.

In my opinion, the biggest reason most investors fail to get truly amazing results is that they ignore the 80% of emotional work that generates the bulk of their results. Instead, they focus all of their attention on the remaining 20% – the technicalities. This is like trying to build a house with just a hammer and without any blueprints or plans!

Sure, it is often easier to immerse yourself in the technical side of things, but the real work is in managing the emotional side of investing, which is what I am concentrating on in this book.

Chapter 10

Good things take time

'We all move through life differently. Some prefer to do as little as possible, others live at full speed.'

Bjarte Bakke

Most people are familiar with the Olympic Games. It's an event that rolls around every four years at which the best athletes from a range of countries compete in different sports in the quest for personal and national glory. The modern Olympic motto is 'Citius, Altius, Fortius', which is Latin for 'Faster, Higher, Stronger'.

Just like the Olympics, I have my own property investing motto: 'Safer, Faster, More Predictably', which translates as 'Tutius, Citius, Praedictio'.

While most people know what the Olympic Games is, far fewer people have a genuine goal to compete at the Olympics. An even smaller number ever actually achieve that goal and only a very tiny number will ever reach the highest sporting peak and come away as an Olympic medal winner.

People like the idea of competing at the Olympics and all the glory that comes with it, but the reality is that most people will never even start the process of doing what it takes to get there. It's just like becoming financially free through property investing.

Most people like the idea and the concept of building the life they desire through property, but only a few will do it, because the gap between where they are now and where they want to be is too big. Beyond that, they simply don't know how to get started. (I cover this more in chapter 14.)

Most people understand what the Olympic Games stands for, but far fewer can genuinely understand what it takes to prepare for the Olympic Games.

There are many parallels that can be drawn between becoming a successful property investor and training for the Olympics. Both pursuits require:

- meticulous planning
- deliberate focus
- significant time to achieve mastery
- a team approach.

Most people don't wake up one day and say, 'I think I'll compete in the Olympics tomorrow, next week or next month'.

Practice makes perfect

In his book *Outliers*, Malcolm Gladwell wrote, 'Ten thousand hours is the magic number of greatness'. This might be a generalisation, but the principle holds that 10,000 hours of 'deliberate practice' are needed to become world-class in any field. And let's make it clear, just going through the motions of doing something is not considered deliberate practice. No, deliberate practice means practising something in a way that pushes your skillset as much as possible.

Think about that. Let's assume you had the time, ability and dedication to deliberately practise something for four hours a day, five days a week, for 50 weeks every year, over the next decade. That would be: 4 x 5 x 50 x 10 = the magical 10,000 hours.

If you did this practice, you would undoubtedly become much better at that task than you are right now. This is especially true of activities where the rules don't change – for example, games such as chess or tennis, where the rules have remained largely the same for hundreds of years.

> **Mentor tip**
> When it comes to property investing, the rules are changing all the time, so even if you had previously committed to those 10,000 hours of practice there is no guarantee that, by using those skillsets today, you would still be able to get to Olympic-level investing in a new economic landscape.

Who has a spare 10,000 hours to deliberately practise anything?

Think about it. If you want to become good at something – and I mean *really* good – few could argue that it is going to take time. For example:

- If you want to become a black-belt in martial arts, depending on which one, you are looking at a minimum of five years' practice (and, in some cases, more like ten).
- To become a master builder in Australia, you will need at least ten years of hands-on experience.
- To become a surgeon generally includes four to six years of medical school and four to six years as a surgical trainee.
- To become an Olympic athlete, you usually need to train for eight years or more to reach the required level to compete.

Studies have found that almost all Olympic athletes started out in their sport at a young age. These athletes were passionate about their sport and also were very good at it, and then they began to put in the time necessary to become great at it.

When it comes to property investing, is it something you are or can get really passionate about? There is no right or wrong answer here. You either enjoy property and the idea of property investing or you don't.

> **#LetsGetReal**
> Success begins with following a passion. In business or investing, or any worthwhile endeavour, it helps to be passionate. It is hard to imagine becoming world-class at anything that you do not love.

If you know you don't but still want to get all the results that successful property investing can provide, then you may simply be better off teaming up with someone who does – someone who has spent the 10,000-plus hours mastering the skills and is willing to share that experience with you.

Even if you are passionate about property investing, there may still be significant advantages in teaming up with more experienced investors until such time as your own experience and results can match your level of passion.

> **Mentor tip**
> Sometimes in life you want to have the satisfaction of doing the work; at other times, you just want the results. For all investors, knowing the difference is a good place to start.

For example, I like having a clean office and coming home to a clean house, but I don't want to spend my own time cleaning, vacuuming and scrubbing toilets. So, I outsource this work to professional cleaners. This makes sense as my time is far better spent on other, higher-order tasks. It is more cost-effective to outsource this to someone who is more passionate about it and has the time and resources to do a better job than I ever would.

How you prioritise your time and select the tasks that you will (or won't) attend to on a regular basis – and the relationship this has to your success – is the subject of the next chapter.

Chapter 11

Is it time?

'You will never find time for anything.
If you want time, you must make it.'

Charles Buxton

In the previous chapter, I spoke about the magic number of 10,000 hours – the amount of time a passionate person will take to become really good at anything. The idea of being able to find five minutes – let alone an extra four hours a day, five days a week, every year for the next decade – to truly master a new skill is paralysing for some people.

These days we all seem to lead very busy lives. Most of us have already made major commitments to our work, families, sports or exercise regimens, hobbies or other worthy pursuits before we even think about scheduling time to master a new skill.

#LetsGetReal

The ability to find even five minutes of clear thinking time every day can be a challenge. For most people, at the end of a long day it's easier to plonk themselves in front of the TV, hit up social media, read a book or simply run a hot bath to help wash away the challenges of the day.

Making more time

If getting better results in the property investment space is important to you then you need to make one of two choices:

1. Learn how to better manage your own time and how to become a full-time professional property investor.
2. Learn how to better leverage other people's time (OPT) to help create the results you want. This is also called outsourcing.

You are probably already outsourcing many things in your life. For example, not too many people try to service their own motor vehicles anymore. These days, new cars are more like computers with wheels – they require a specialised level of knowledge and tools to perform the job. So it is usually easier, and makes more sense, to pay a qualified mechanic to service your car rather than try to do it yourself.

Outsourcing makes sense in a number of ways. You should seriously consider outsourcing a task if any or all of the following holds true:

- Someone else can perform the task better, faster or more cost-effectively than you can.
- You don't have the time or desire to become a master of the task in the timeframe available to you.
- You value your time more than the financial cost of having the task performed by someone else.
- You want to create opportunities of employment for other people.

Understanding how you spend or invest your time

Working smarter does not mean having to work longer hours. Not surprisingly, one of the most popular topics in the self-help and personal development fields is time management.

There are literally thousands of books and articles on time management, giving information that is designed to help you better allocate how and where you spend your most finite resource of all – time.

For some people, it is like a badge of honour to tell the world how busy they are, or how little they sleep, or how they are using the latest tool, app or technology to optimise their time.

But are you really as busy as you think?

I want to illustrate a couple of vitally important points about time management. Let's start with a little story about a university professor who wanted to teach his students about time management. He a created a lesson plan that went like this.

A lesson in time management

Standing out in front of the class, the professor reached under the lectern and pulled out a large, empty glass jar. He proceeded to fill it with big rocks until no more rocks could fit inside the jar. He asked the class if the jar was full.

Some students agreed that it was, but others decided that it would be possible to fit something smaller in between the gaps that existed between the big rocks.

So the professor reached down below the lectern and brought out a bag of small pebbles and poured as many as he could into the jar, filling all the gaps between the big rocks.

Again, he asked the class if the jar was full. This time, a few more students agreed that the jar was full, but a few still had doubts.

The professor reached below once more and brought out a tray of sand, which he proceeded to pour into the jar, filling all the holes that the students could see through the glass.

When is the jar full?

Again, he asked the class if the jar was full. Even more students now agreed the jar was full, but a few were still not sure. So the professor reached below the lectern once again and brought out a container of water. He then proceeded to pour water into the jar with the large rocks, the pebbles and the sand until the jar was overflowing.

Everyone now agreed that the jar was in fact full (except for a few quantum physics nerds, who still argued that it was more empty space than full at an atomic level).

Now the professor asked the most important question of the lesson: 'What is the moral of this story?'

The students thought hard about this, discussed it among themselves and finally came up with their answer. Susan was elected to be the group spokesperson and proudly proclaimed, 'The moral of the story is that you can always fit more in'.

The professor smiled to himself because he knew that the class was about to receive a very valuable lesson on time management.

'Thanks Susan, and thank you class for that response, but unfortunately that is not the moral we are looking for here', the professor explained.

'Instead, imagine for a moment that I reversed the order to how we filled the jar. Instead of starting with the big rocks, imagine I poured in the exact same volume of water first, followed by the exact same amount of sand, and the same number of small pebbles. Now what would happen to the big rocks?' the professor asked his eager students.

Then the penny dropped and Susan blurted, 'They wouldn't all be able to fit in the jar!'

'Exactly', the professor said.

The moral of this story is that when it comes to time management, you need to start with the most important things. Or, in other words, start with the big rocks.

Ask a busy person

Have you ever heard the saying, 'If you want something done, ask a busy person'? What does that actually mean? Well, there a couple of different ways to think about it.

First, busy people could be seen as efficient, reliable and effective, with a good sense of how long things should take to complete. They may be focused on producing results and completing tasks. Given their experience in getting lots done, they know how much they can fit into any given day or week and how much they've currently got on their plates. If they take something on, it's because they have thought about how long it will take, they have looked at the amount of time they have available and they have calculated that it will work.

> 'Your time is limited, so don't waste it living someone else's life... Don't let the noise of others' opinions drown out your own inner voice. And, most important, have the courage to follow your heart and intuition.'
>
> *Steve Jobs*

Or, if you think about it in another way, busy people are busy because they have never taken the time to work out what is important to them and do not have the ability to say no to things or tasks, irrespective of whether they should be doing them or not.

#LetsGetReal
Being busy for busy's sake can lead to all sorts of issues, including severe burnout. The human machine is amazing, but it is not indefatigable. Pushing yourself further and harder is rarely the best solution and, in fact, the lessons in this book are designed to help you do less and achieve more.

Just taking on more and more without a clear purpose or plan is likely to result in a string of unfinished or poorly completed tasks and activities. This can lead to a sense of failure and, if not corrected, it can cause a cascading effect of ever-worsening outcomes, which results in a complete sense of hopelessness and giving up on your dreams.

Can you relate to any of this? What dreams have you given up on, not because they are no longer important to you but because you haven't found a way to make them happen?

Finally, if you're too busy, it means that you may be spending too much time on the wrong things in your life. Efficiency and effectiveness are often two different things. We can try and become as efficient as we like, but if we are allocating our time to the wrong areas of our life it will be largely ineffective.

Better time management has nothing to do with time and everything to do with your priorities!

Time is actually fairly easy to work with, at least mathematically. We each have 60 minutes in an hour, 24 hours in a day, 7 days in a week and 52 weeks in a year.

> **#LetsGetReal**
> Instead of spending all your time complaining about how busy you are, have you ever stopped and asked yourself, 'How is it that other people can appear to get so much more done in the same 7 days in a week that I have?'

The most productive people I know spend more time thinking about WHAT to work on as opposed to HOW to work on them. Lower-productivity people do exactly the opposite – blindly working on HOW to get things done without first deciding WHAT is worth their time. In other words, you can become highly efficient, but if you're working on the wrong things it doesn't matter how efficient you are.

How to become more effective

> 'If the ladder is not leaning against the right wall, every step we take just gets us to the wrong place faster.'
>
> *Stephen R. Covey*

Let me offer a few practical solutions to help you become more *effective*, not more *efficient*, with your time and make your time on this planet more rewarding.

Remember, there are only 24 hours in a day and 7 days in a week. That cannot change. What can change is how, or on what, you choose to spend that time. The problem for most people is that they have never sat down and worked out what their priorities actually are. (More on this in chapter 13.)

#LetsGetReal

I strongly encourage you to conduct an audit of how you are currently spending your time. Remember, at this stage I am not making any judgments or seeking to change anything you are doing. I'm just asking you to make an honest appraisal of how you are currently spending your time. This exercise could be a real eye-opener for you!

Take a few minutes to think about all the things you do on a regular basis. Start by making a list and allocating how much time you think you currently spend on each task. Let's use the period of a week to start with, as it is long enough to accommodate the activities that we don't do daily but still do on a regular basis.

Activity	No. of hours/week Current	No. of hours/week Ideal

It is up to you to decide on your big rocks, pebbles, sand and water. If I asked 100 random people what the three most important things were in their lives, I would likely get many different responses. Generally speaking, most people would define things such as their health, family and friends as 'big rocks'.

How do you spend your time?

To get you thinking about how much time you spend on your big rocks, let's take health as an example.

Big Rock: Health

You probably know how much **sleep** you need to operate well and enjoy optimal levels of health and wellbeing. For this exercise, I want you to think about and write down some details about how much sleep you are currently getting per week and what you should ideally be aiming for.

Current: ___ *hours*
Ideal: ___ *hours*

How much sleep (or time in bed) did you enjoy last night?

I went to bed at ___ am/pm
I fell asleep at around ___ am/pm
I woke up at ___ am/pm
I got up at ___ am/pm.
Is that normal for you? Yes/No
Is that optimal you? Yes/No

Next, **food**. Consider all aspects of eating here, including time spent shopping, preparing meals and going to and from places to eat out as well as the time you actually spend eating. Again, this is an average weekly figure over the course of the year. So, if you only eat out once a month but spend four hours doing it, that might account for an average of one hour per week.

Current: ___ hours
Ideal: ___ hours

Time spent engaged in **sports and exercise** includes time spent getting to and from where you train or exercise. This could include incidental activities such as walking the dog or gardening.

Current: ___ hours
Ideal: ___ hours

Average out your weekly health hours and tally them up to get your **Big Rock subtotal**.

Current: ___ hours
Ideal: ___ hours

Next, let's look at another common big rock – time spent with friends and family.

Big Rock: Friends and family

How much time do you currently spend on **quality family time**? Make sure you don't double up. For example, don't include the time spent eating dinner with your family here if you have already allocated that time above in the food section.

Current: ___ hours
Ideal: ___ hours

Next, note the time you spend deliberately building your most important **romantic relationship(s)**, with clear time away from the kids, work, day-to-day monotony and other distractions. This is where you note the amount of time spent in sexual intimacy (as well as the time spent thinking about it). While I have listed this in 'hours', I appreciate that some may need to log this in minutes.

Current: ___ hours
Ideal: ___ hours

Next, **social activities**. This could be time spent at specific events, some of which will be known in advance, such as birthdays and work Christmas parties. You can also include events that you may not know about in advance, such as weddings and funerals. You can choose to include family time, hanging out with friends and maybe even time spent on Facebook or Instagram here if this is truly important to you.

Current: ___ hours
Ideal: ___ hours

Average out your weekly social obligations and desires and tally it all up to get your **Big Rock subtotal**.

Current: ___ hours
Ideal: ___ hours

Mentor tip
What you consistently spend the most time doing is high on your priority list and vice versa.

Most people do what is most important to them

You will subconsciously spend the most time doing those things that are most important to you. So, if you say that family is the most important thing to you but you spend every waking hour at work, then I am sorry but family is not actually your highest priority – work is.

If you say that health is your number-one priority and you don't eat well or haven't exercised since primary school, then I am sorry, health is not among your highest priorities. Let's get real – we are being honest with ourselves after all, right?

Interestingly, often things such as work and wealth creation don't make the big rocks category at all. Is it any wonder then that many people don't get the best results from their investing? It simply isn't that important to them when all is said and done.

If this is true for you, then a major tip I can give you is to find as many ways as possible to link your investment success to what is most important to you. For example, if you said that your highest priority is health, how can creating more money from your investing help you with that?

Well, with more access to personal wealth, you could take on a personal trainer, buy better-quality foods, and get massages and other health treatments more frequently.

Go and work out what your lower-order values and priorities should be by deciding what activities go in your pebbles, sand and water categories. For example, you might choose to prioritise the pleasure and relaxation you get by watching TV (including Foxtel, Netflix, Stan or other on-demand streaming platforms) as a pebble. Or perhaps you rarely watch any TV, and this time would be better categorised as water.

Mentor tip
Linking the outcome of your investment success to your highest priority greatly enhances your motivation to succeed in your investing.

To make this process easier for you, I have created a bonus resource to help guide you through this exercise. This resource will help you identify what is truly important to you and act as both a record for where you are currently at and a reference over time to help you track your priorities in life. Head over to www.thepropertymentors.com.au/myAtoB and get real with yourself today.

Goal-setting exercises like this one that encourage you to think about your life can be daunting for some people. They often fear these exercises because they do not have a history of success with them. Some people have never gone through this process – it is not commonly taught at home, in school or in the workplace. Others have spent countless hours designing dream boards or writing down goals, often with no tangible results to show for it at the end of the day. Given these poor results, they now shun the thought of doing yet more of something they view as a fruitless exercise.

A better way to approach anything you have not tried before or tried without luck, is to not just give up on the process. Instead, try something different until you achieve a better result. That is why having an experienced mentor in your corner is invaluable, as what works for one person may not work for another.

#LetsGetReal

If you haven't done the aforementioned exercise, let's get real – do it. It is a valuable process to go through and a good investment of your time.

PART II

IT'S ALL ABOUT YOU

Congratulations on reading this far in the book. I've asked you a lot of questions already and hope you have been honest with your answers. It's time to get real, remember? In this second part of the book, I continue to guide you to look further into yourself to discover what you really want and how you can achieve it.

Chapter 12

Do you mind if we discuss your mindset?

'Once you replace negative thoughts with positive ones, you'll start having positive results.'

Willie Nelson

Remember in chapter 9 when you confirmed that there were probably people in your line of work who were doing better than you? Those individuals became more successful than you largely because their WHY was likely to have been bigger than yours.

Going back to the analogy in chapter 2, they had a stronger motivation to reach the other side of the lake than you did. They were probably willing to do more than you to get to the other side. They were not necessarily better swimmers or started across the lake any earlier than you, they just knew WHY getting to the other side of the lake was important to them and took action to do something about it.

At some point in their past, they made the decision to prioritise various aspects of their life and put themselves into a position to attract a higher level of success in those particular areas.

You may want to be a successful property investor, but there is something missing, or you would have already achieved all the results you wanted by now. This chapter discovers what that could be.

> **#LetsGetReal**
> If your WHY is big enough, the HOW TO will take care of itself.

It takes more than skill to succeed

You might be surprised to discover that you need more than just skills to achieve your goals. Some of the top tertiary-educated students come out of university with all the skills they need but find there is no job waiting for them on the other side.

I have seen first-hand the struggles law graduates face to get a job in the legal profession – after all those years at university! To get into a half-decent law firm these days, you really have to be the best of the best. All the students who miss out on a graduate position still have the skillset they need to get one of these prized positions, but unfortunately the skills alone are not enough. There is no shortage of degree-qualified baristas and retail workers out there to prove this!

Accessing the right information

Having the right skills is never enough, because it is not too difficult to learn the skills to undertake almost any endeavour. Take flying an aircraft, for example. Flying a plane of any size is a pretty serious business. If you stuff it up you could kill yourself, or others, in addition to ruining a perfectly good plane. But it is *possible* to become an airline pilot. Around the world, tens of thousands of people become licensed pilots each year. If you want to learn how to fly a plane, the information required to do so is available.

It's possible that you could learn how to fly by watching YouTube videos, googling instructions, visiting a library and borrowing some books on the subject. You could talk to an experienced pilot or even watch *Air Crash Investigations* (and then hopefully just do the opposite!).

However, if you are serious and really want to become a pilot, you wouldn't just jump on Google, read internet forums, talk to friends and family and read the latest newspaper to find out how to do it, would you? This is serious stuff, man!

The point I'm making here is that it is not merely access to (the right) information that is important, it is how that information is even relevant to where you are at right now.

Where do you start? How do you know which bits of information are crucial and which is just information for information's sake? How do all the separate bits of information actually tie together?

There would be little point in learning all about how to land a plane if you haven't even learned how to take off! That's an obvious one, of course, but how would you know if you should study how to calculate and assess fuel loads first, or study weather patterns? Without industry experience or expert guidance, you probably wouldn't even know how or where to start.

So, if it's not just about learning a skill and finding the right information relevant to your own situation, then what else is missing?

Getting out of your comfort zone

As I discussed earlier in the book, you'll need to be prepared to go out of your comfort zone if you want to achieve your goals and ultimate success.

Think for a minute what the term 'comfort zone' really means. It's an area that you are comfortable in of course. Being comfortable means that you are not really challenged in any way, and that you are familiar with your surroundings.

Someone in their comfort zone, for example, goes to work every day, comes home, watches TV, eats dinner and goes to bed, and does the same thing day in and day out with no real change. From the outside, they appear to be drifting through life and not really moving forward. Sure, they may be a nice, 'normal' person, but they never do anything to really challenge themselves to take their results to the next level. Do you know anyone like this?

There are always going to be people like this, and that is okay. While I would love to help everyone build a better life, and I aspire to help as many people as possible, it's hard to help someone who doesn't want to help themselves. These people typically, for whatever reason, haven't found a strong enough reason to want to change their lives in any significant way. They may have lost their mojo, or perhaps they have just fallen into bad habits, or they don't think they can do more with their lives. They may think they can't afford to take any risks.

Whatever the reason, it is as if they have fallen into quicksand and have been told not to struggle for fear of drowning even faster. So they just wait there, sinking slowly, waiting for death to envelop them. In fact, the only way they will be able to get out of the quicksand is for someone to throw them a lifeline, or in some other way wake up from their dreamy state and stop drifting through life.

It's all in the mind

People go out and make massive financial decisions, such as buying an investment property, by simply searching the internet for what to do. They believe all the media articles and, even worse, they listen to advice from their friends and family, even if they don't have any real experience or results in the space! By taking this approach they are probably lucky to get even an average result. This approach to investing is mostly based on luck and not skill.

I acknowledged earlier that it is possible to learn how to fly a plane by researching on the internet – possible, but foolhardy. The plane could crash, resulting in a catastrophic, grisly mess. Having a disastrous experience in property investing is not as bad as crashing a plane and dying; instead, it could send you broke.

So, what is the missing ingredient?

I may be harping on about it, but your mindset is one of the most fundamental determinants of your success in any field.

Flowchart for success

If I had to provide a simple flow for success it would be this:

Quite simply, your Thoughts combine with your lived experience to create your Beliefs.

These Beliefs then determine what Actions (or inaction) you will take in any situation.

The sum of all those Actions then creates your Results in life.

So, if there is some result you want to change in your life, where should you focus to change those results? Most people make the mistake of focusing all their energy on the actions (learning the skills) or the result (flying the plane), not on what creates the results – their mindset!

This book is all about creating the platform for investors to change their results by identifying the Thoughts, Beliefs and Actions that created their results in the first place.

It's easy to talk about this, and intellectually many of you have probably been nodding your heads in agreement as you have progressed through this book.

#LetsGetReal
Holding a mirror up to your own life and taking 100% responsibility for all the thoughts, beliefs, actions and results can be HARD WORK!

It often takes enormous amounts of courage and personal discipline to hold yourself to account in this way. Perhaps that is why very few people tackle this issue, or only give it lip service at best.

Very few people want to accept that their entire outer world is largely a manifestation of their most inner thoughts and beliefs. For those who do, the challenge is to keep improving this skill year on year.

Until you can make that shift and embrace this process, you will forever be limited in what you can achieve. Mastering your thoughts, moulding your beliefs and taking smarter action are the only sure-fire ways to change your results. As I have said throughout this book, this process of self-discovery is not going to be easy for everyone, but the rewards are there for those who succeed.

So, the next time you start to feel any fear, doubt or indecision, catch yourself and stop.

Start by identifying the negative thought processes. Pay attention to your thoughts and consider where they came from. This can be challenging at first, and you may find yourself subconsciously resisting this course of action, but persist, because this is part of the learning process as you grow. It takes time and dedicated practice to learn anything new.

It is normal to feel some discomfort; it often won't feel right at first, but the more you do it the more comfortable it becomes.

You aren't going to change in one day or one week, but little by little you'll go far!

Remember, Perth wasn't built in a day, so above all else be patient with yourself, look for all the little wins along the way and celebrate all your progress, no matter how big or small.

Mentor tip
Be nice to yourself and look for ways to build yourself up, instead of excuses to beat yourself up.

Chapter 13

She'll be right, mate...

'Planning is bringing the future into the present, so that you can do something about it now.'

Alan Lakein

Australians are a pretty laid-back bunch. We tend to take things in our stride and have even coined the phrase 'She'll be right, mate' to indicate that everything will work out in the end. And if we are lucky, maybe it will. After all, Australia is the lucky country, right? To date, property has proven to be a pretty forgiving mistress in Australia. It has been easy for many property investors and owner occupiers to just sit back and enjoy the ride.

Over the last 30 years, according to CoreLogic data, the combined capital city dwelling values have increased by 453.1%, with noticeable falls only during the GFC and the COVID-19 pandemic – see Figure 1.

Over the last 10 years (which includes the period of the COVID-19 pandemic), prices still returned an average 7.2%, says Tim Lawless, Research Director at CoreLogic Australia. But do you really want to pin the rest of your life on luck and an optimistic viewpoint?

No? In that case, read on.

Figure 1: Change in combined capital city dwelling values over the last 30 years

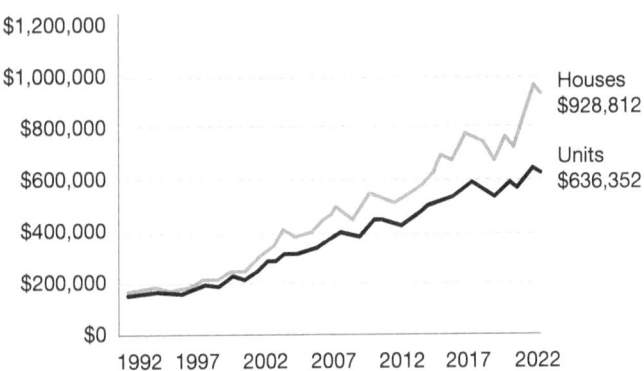

Source: CoreLogic

You need a plan

Most people wouldn't start a long journey without planning it first. There are lots of things to consider and being prepared can prevent things going horribly wrong, or prevent you simply ending up in the wrong place.

For example, let's assume you want to go on an off-road, four-wheel driving adventure. You'll be venturing out into the middle of nowhere. It's not enough to simply arrive at your destination – much of the fun is in actually getting there!

You see, when you leave a sealed road and start driving on a track, everything changes. You leave behind the comforts of safe driving conditions and having other road users nearby to lend a hand if you break down, get a flat tyre or run out of fuel.

When you make that first turn off the sealed road, it can be exciting, but the thing about off-road tracks is that often they aren't used for days, weeks or months at a time. If they run through the bush, there could be fallen trees, huge potholes and rivers in the way, and sometimes the track may have simply been washed away altogether. This uncertainty brings a whole new set of challenges, and you have to think on your feet when you come up against an obstacle.

You can prepare for an off-road journey by thinking about your equipment and all the things that could go wrong:

- Is your vehicle in good condition?
- Has it been serviced recently?
- Are the tyres capable of surviving the journey, and do you have a spare tyre (or two)?
- Do you have enough fuel or a long-range tank?
- Do you have a jerry can with some backup fuel?
- Have you got adequate supplies of food or water, or tools to find them if you need to?
- What about a basic toolkit to make repairs?
- Do you even know how to repair your vehicle if you get stuck?
- What about river crossings? Do you know how to safely cross the river? What if you get stuck?
- If you come across a fallen tree over the track, 100 km away from the nearest sealed road, do you have the right equipment to get it out of your way or cut through it?
- What if you hit a section of the track that is muddy and you get stuck?

These are just some of the considerations, but on top of these there are so many factors to consider that you need to be aware of. The 'she'll be right' approach could turn your little off-road adventure into an off-road nightmare!

Don't panic!

Australia is a massive country. While city folk are used to having good roads, almost 100% mobile phone coverage, fast internet access and help nearby, in rural areas you don't have the creature comforts that we have become accustomed to.

For example, in the bush, if you are 100 km away from the nearest sealed road and your vehicle gets stuck, you will have no phone signal, and even on CB radio you might not be able to make contact for some time. You may have limited food on board and not much water. You will have to deal with weather conditions and even wild animals that might want to eat, bite or sting you. Things can escalate pretty quickly in these types of emergency situations because people panic.

When people panic, their rational and logical thinking goes out the window and emotion takes over. It's human nature, and it has been proven time and time again when swimmers get swept out to sea, panic and end up drowning.

Even experienced off-road drivers can find themselves in sticky situations, but the most experienced have learned over time exactly what to look out for, what to pack and how to best prepare the vehicle for the challenge ahead. Time and time again it is the inexperienced who typically get caught in situations that could have been avoided or better handled.

It's no different with investing

They say a journey of a thousand miles starts with a single step, and most people see that as a call to action to get started on their investing journey – but it should really start with a plan. Even with a plan, there will be challenges along the way as the image overleaf shows. Reality rarely goes according to plan.

They say failing to plan is planning to fail, yet so few people take the time to plan out their investment journey. I travel all around Australia educating Australians on how to get better results from property investing. I frequently ask the audience, 'Who here has written down a clear wealth plan mapping out how they are going to create the financial results they desire and by when?'

I am lucky if one or two people in a room of any size admit that they have one. And even then, when pressed, their plan may not actually be written down. They assure me that it is in their heads and they know what they want to achieve. Yeah, right, let's get real!

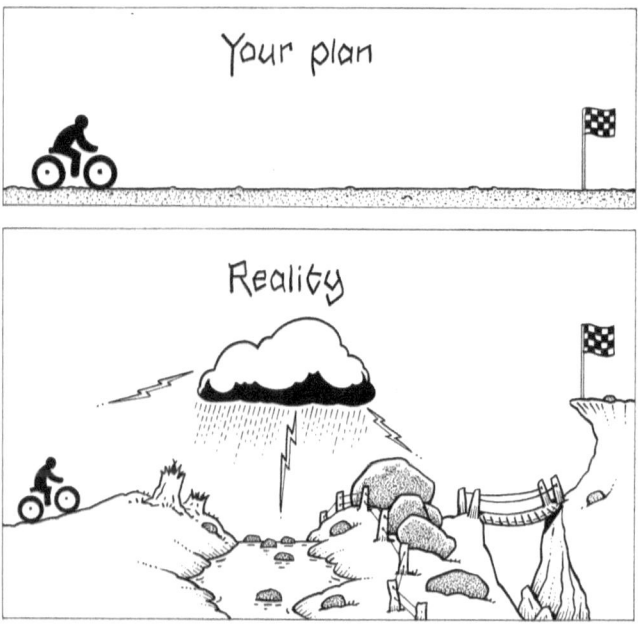

I am not having a go at anyone here, but seriously, it speaks volumes as to the priorities of some people. They spend more time organising the songs on Spotify, watching cat videos on YouTube or posting comments on social media than they do organising their actual lives. So, why is that?

#LetsGetReal
I know first-hand that the 'she'll be right' approach simply doesn't work.

Now that I've brought this issue to the surface, you can probably see that some of your priorities have become messed up along the way. There are usually two reasons for this:

1. Life planning, goal-setting or whatever you want to call it is not something that comes naturally. It is rarely taught at home or at school, or learned first and then mastered.
2. You can't start to plan out something if you don't even know what you want in life, and often nobody has ever really challenged you to think about what you want from your life in any real detail.

Are you willing to admit to yourself that you have probably been guilty of failing to plan your investing and your life effectively? And even if you have attempted planning in the past, are you open to the idea that there might be a better way to do it?

If you're ready to do something about it, then please keep reading, because the rubber is about to really hit the road!

Chapter 14

Planning your road map to success

'When the student is ready... the lesson appears.'

Gene Oliver

Congratulations on reading this far. Investing is a long-term proposition, and there is a lot to learn; so hang in there and stay focused, because I think that a great life is worth working towards over the long term.

Interestingly, according to a report by the Financial Planning Association and social research group McCrindle, 63% of people surveyed had no plan, or only a very loose plan, for how they were going to achieve their financial goals. The research further discovered that 47% of people regretted they had not saved more, 34% wished they had spent less and only 27% thought they could have invested more.

#LetsGetReal
When it comes to planning, one of the most effective questions you can ask yourself is: 'Is what I am doing right now going to get me closer to, or further away from, what I am trying to achieve?'

You need to ask this question of yourself in your decision-making processes every day. It can be applied to every decision you make every day.

If you want to get that beach body for summer, is that burger combo and sugar-filled drink going to get you closer to your goal of being ripped and hot for summer, or is it pushing you further away?

Is getting mad, or staying mad, at your partner for some trivial, perceived indiscretion taking you closer to your goal of a happy and loving relationship or further away from it?

Ask yourself the question – whatever the situation. It's a great way of being accountable to yourself and your goals. Write it down and stick it up on the fridge as a great little daily reminder.

In the context of investing, this question is even more relevant. If a particular investment opportunity doesn't get you closer to your goals, why would you buy it?

As discussed previously, most investors don't even know what their goals are in the first place. But, jumping forward and assuming you now have goals in place, asking this simple yet powerful question can help keep you on track and motivated to achieve your goals.

Defining your Point A

Defining your road map to success starts with establishing where you are right now, and owning all the decisions and thought processes that you have gone through to get you to this point in your life.

I call where you are in life right now your 'Point A' position, and where you want to get to I call your 'Point B' position.

> **Mentor tip**
> Ninety-nine per cent of people out there have never really stopped to think about this in any great detail. If you can master this, you are in the 1%.

Most people have good intentions, of course, but they are drifting through life. They have never been challenged to review where they are in life and how they got here. They assume that getting to their end destination is going to be smooth sailing, or that you can get there by simply drifting.

> **#LetsGetReal**
> Before we discuss your goals and how we set out your plan, let's discuss where you are right now in life. Let's review how you got to where you are and what decisions you made to get to this point in your financial and personal life.

Know where you are heading

> *'Stress is caused by being "here" but wanting to be "there".'*
>
> Eckhart Tolle

Imagine for a moment that you live in Sydney and you want to go to Perth. You have decided to drive because, after all, you recognise that it's as important to enjoy the journey as it is to arrive at your destination. Now, after you have made the conscious decision to head to Perth, you have to decide if you want to just get in the car and wing it, hoping you make it there, or if you want to get there in a more predictable way.

You would never expect to head out of your driveway and simply end up in Perth without at least knowing which direction to go in. Yet, with investing, people just go out there and start investing without establishing a clear destination first. This is the equivalent of just jumping in the car and hoping you can navigate your way there by luck, or perhaps by following someone who looks like they might be heading to Perth.

Sure, you are ultimately going to end up somewhere, but it may not be where you wanted to go. You may get distracted and end up somewhere completely different! Having a GPS will most certainly help you get to your destination safer, faster and more predictably.

You can simply punch in the destination and press 'start journey' with a high level of confidence that the GPS is going to show you the fastest and safest way to get there.

Right now, I challenge you to visualise jumping into a helicopter with me and flying up to take a big-picture view of your life and where you are at right now. There's no need to panic, I do this all the time, so you're in safe hands!

Next, grab the biggest sheet of paper you can find and your favourite pen, pencil or crayon and start writing out where you are right now. (I prefer to use an A3 sheet of paper, or bigger, so you can make a huge, fun mess of it! Don't use spreadsheets, they are boring.)

On the left side of the paper, write a big A, and on the right side a big B.

A   B

While I agree in part with Eckhart Tolle's quote earlier, I think there's something missing. I prefer to say, 'Stress is caused by being "here" but wanting to be "there"... *and not knowing how to bridge the gap*'.

So let's – metaphorically at least – bridge the gap.

Now draw a line between the A and the B. This is the connection between where you are now and where you want to be.

Now, let's get back to A. I want you to get real here and think about the answers to these questions:

- How much money do you have in your bank accounts right now?
- What is the total of all your assets (including superannuation, property, shares, etc.)?
- What is the total of all your liabilities (including credit cards, mortgages, car loans, etc.)?
- What is your income (or your combined income if you are a couple)?
- How much free time do you have?
- How many hours a week are you working?
- Are you living the life you desire?
- Do you travel enough?
- When was your last holiday and where did you go? Are there other destinations that you have ruled out because you can't afford it or don't have the time to get away?
- Do you spend enough quality time with your family and friends?
- Are you driving the car you want?
- Are you donating to charity and giving back to the world?
- Are you emotionally rewarded doing what you are doing with your life?
- Are you happy, truly happy, doing what you are doing with your life?
- Are you fulfilled?

- Are you happy in your relationship or just hanging in there because it's comfortable?
- Is your health what you want it to be?
- If you had to stop work right now, how long would your money last?
- If your life were to end tomorrow, could you be proud of all you have accomplished during your time on the planet? Or have you left some fuel in the tank?

#LetsGetReal
Answer the questions listed above and summarise your answers under the A on your sheet of paper.

(I know that often when you read books like this you keep reading and don't do the activities, because you don't know how or why they are relevant. Believe me, this is super important, so go grab that paper now if you haven't already done so and start writing down the answers to the questions below the A.)

A  **B**

Bank account $15K
All assets $700K
Liabilities $250K
Income $150K

Mentor tip
I realise that for some people this process can be confronting – and so it should be. Look for ways to embrace this process, though, as this could be just the wake-up call or kick up the bum that you need to get your finances back on track, or turbo-charged to even greater heights.

Be accountable

The reason some individuals find this process challenging is because in most people's lives it is rare to be confronted with these things directly. Most people like to skirt around difficult conversations and put things off for another day. Well, as the saying goes, 'Someday is not a day of the week'.

It can feel odd to have these questions asked so directly, and you may not have an emotional strategy in place to deal with this just yet. But please just work through all your feelings and reconcile yourself to the fact that you are going to go through the process, so you might as well embrace the change. As I said earlier in the book, the sooner we can get to the middle of the lake, the quicker we can get to the other side.

The thought of actually having to put the answers down in writing, and then to be accountable for all the results in your life, can be overwhelming for some – especially if deep down you know you could have, and probably should have, done more with your life to date.

Most investors never write down their goals because they don't see the point, and those who do aren't accountable to anyone, so the list of goals sits on the fridge until they get frustrated and put it in a drawer. Even those who are accountable to someone (such as their partner) still usually give up or lose focus over time as 'life' invariably gets in the way.

Modern society does not provide a template for assessing your life and whether you are on track or not. We are not born with a manual or guidebook for success that, if we just follow it, will assure us an amazing life.

When you stop studying and enter the adult world, you are largely left to fend for yourself. Most adults never make the conscious connection that they are no longer a child and they are in FULL control of their destiny.

The majority of the population falls neatly into the system that has been carefully designed for them. They go out and get a job, pay their taxes and try to be good little citizens. That's what they were taught to do; that's why they were sent to school for all those years, or why some went on to university to further their education. It's all about going to school and getting that job to make money. People just accept this as the normal process, and that's what they end up doing.

Then they're expected to save up to buy a house and have kids. Then they get old and die. You see, people aren't taught how to build wealth through the education system, so if you want to be educated on wealth creation you must deliberately go out there and find that education yourself.

Now, I'm not discounting the hard work, effort and dedication that people put into their school or tertiary education, and I know that there are many successful people who have gone above and beyond what most achieve by working in a job. The reality is, however, if you are trading hours for dollars in a job or business – regardless of your income – it's going to be quite difficult to achieve financial independence or build long-term sustainable wealth unless you are leveraging your money.

You get to choose

But that, friends, is not the way it has to be. You are only on this planet ONE TIME. You don't get a second chance at this life. So, I am telling you right now, even if you only take *one thing* from this book, know this – you can't do it again. You won't get today back.

People get used to the fact that the sun will rise tomorrow and tomorrow is 'just another day' on this earth, but forget that we are all here for a finite period of time. The clock is always ticking.

You go through your twenties and get to 30 so fast you barely even realise it has happened. It seems like just yesterday you were a teenager, and now you're one of those 30-somethings – wow! Then, before you know it, your thirties are gone too and your forties begin. Next thing you know, you are old and grey!

Guys and gals, time is so precious; your life is over in an instant, so make the most of every bit of it. Don't waste your time doing a job you hate, being in a relationship that isn't working or waking up each day and hating life because of where you are at.

Take a good look at your current situation and ask yourself if you're happy with your results and whether you could have done things any differently or any better. If you are not happy, then you can make some changes – you have a choice!

Okay, so let's get real. Think of one thing in your life right now that you are not happy with and write it down. YOU and only you have the power to change it, so if you don't do it now, when are you going to?

Chapter 15

Defining your Point B

*'If you do not change direction,
you may end up where you are heading.'*

Lao Tzu

Compiling your list under Point A in the previous chapter should have provided you with a reality check. The exercise isn't designed to be another chance to beat yourself up but an opportunity to build yourself back up. This is all about getting real. If you can't get real about where you are in your life, how can you possibly move forward in the direction of your dreams?

In this chapter, we work on finding your Point B, and this involves thinking about your goals.

The good part about your goals is that they are yours, and yours alone. You, and only you, can make the decision whether you wish to pursue them or not.

If you have made it this far, you are obviously serious about living your ideal life and you want to build a kickass property portfolio. This is a good time to remind you that when I talk of building a successful property portfolio, it means different things for different people. Some people don't need to build a multi-million-dollar portfolio; they will achieve their goals with a much smaller portfolio. What I teach, however, applies to everyone, regardless of the size of their dreams and goals.

It's not about the money

As a general rule, it is not money that people want. What most people want is enough money to allow them the time and financial resources to enjoy the type of lifestyle that they desire. Great, so 99.9% of people want more time and more money to do the things that they really enjoy. So why, then, do so few actually achieve it?

Why you want to invest is actually something that you really need to think about. Investing is not easy; there will be good times and there will be bad times. There may be times when you have cash flow issues; problems with your property manager; tenants to deal with; external factors such as personal issues, work problems or health challenges; or one of a thousand other things that will test your patience for investing.

It is often during the not-so-good times that a lot of investors pack up and go home. They sell their property investments and do something else, hoping for something easier or something to achieve their goals faster.

This is when people dive into something they don't understand, trying to make that elusive quick buck. Making a quick buck is actually possible with property, but it takes planning and careful research and effort to achieve that result. In reality, while it may look like a quick buck to people on the outside, often it has only been possible because of all the background work that has gone into getting yourself ready to identify that opportunity and then make that buck quickly.

#LetsGetReal
Trying to make a quick buck in property with little skill, experience or resources is a risky business. You may just as quickly send yourself broke trying.

To be a successful long-term property investor and to build wealth for your future, you need to understand a few fundamentally important things first. So, while what I will teach you here is by no means new, when it is applied to building wealth through property it is an amazing strategy for success.

What do you want to achieve?

You'll recall from the previous chapter that your starting point is your Point A position and where you want to get to is your Point B position.

It's time now to go back to your sheet of A3 paper and start writing down under B a bunch of things that you want to achieve, no matter how large or small and in no particular order. Do not limit yourself here; this is extremely important. I always encourage people to think big and write down everything. Remember that these are YOUR goals, nobody else's. You don't need to discuss them with your parents, or your cousin, or next-door neighbour – unless you really want to.

> **Mentor tip**
> Your journey begins when, and only when, you get real with yourself about where you are in life. Once you accept that what you have been doing hasn't given you all the results you desire, then and only then can you make a change and move forward.

For a bit of inspiration, here is a short list of things that The Property Mentors' members over the years have told us they want to achieve in their lives:

- cooking classes in Italy
- skydiving on their 50th wedding anniversary
- buying a beach house
- spending more time with the kids

- getting married in Thailand
- helping the kids buy a property
- travelling overseas once a year
- donating money to charity
- replacing the car every three years
- taking the kids to Disneyland
- being fit and healthy
- not having to worry about money
- having the latest gadgets
- not being time poor
- having the freedom do what they want when they want to
- growing old with their partner
- going on fishing trips with the boys
- travelling around Australia in a caravan
- seeing the northern lights
- going to Antarctica
- writing a novel
- paying cash for their next car
- having a cleaner, someone to do the ironing and a gardener
- buying a property in the country
- learning how to make wine
- watching the sunset on the beach
- taking the kids to visit Santa at the North Pole
- putting the kids through private schools
- looking after family in their older years
- taking their partner to fancy restaurants without worrying about the cost.

This is not an exhaustive list by any means, but it provides a starting point for you to ask yourself WHY you are here in the first place. WHY are you investing, and WHY do you even get up and go to work every day right now?

Think big

Try to think big here. Think about all the things you have ever wanted in life. You need to consider all the possibilities and not restrict your thinking to what you think you can do based on your current levels of education, experience or resources. The challenge for most adults is that they have gone through a process of dismissing their goals as they get knocked about in life. Ask a six-year-old what they want to be when they grow up and they will tell you. They have big dreams and goals, and nothing is impossible. They don't place restrictions on what they can and cannot do. Just talking to kids about their future and their big goals often gives adults a buzz of excitement and without knowing it, subconsciously, we relive that feeling that has been missing for all these years.

I challenge you to make your Point B list as comprehensive as possible – and keep growing it in the days and weeks ahead. Note also that this list is not just about financial goals. When I ask people what their dreams are, they tell me they want ten properties in ten years, because they assume I am asking about their financial goals. The financial goals lie underneath the personal goals, not the other way around.

> #LetsGetReal
> Can you achieve all the things on your B list? Absolutely. Will you achieve all these things? Maybe.

Now take a look back at the left of your list, your current Point A position; then take a look to the right, your Point B position. There's a gap between the two, isn't there? And you've drawn a line to fill the gap between where you are now and where you want to be. That line represents the missing link and therefore will become your virtual road map to help you get there in the years ahead.

A ——————————————— B

Bank account $15K	Buying a beach house
All assets $700K	Spending more time with the kids
Liabilities $250K	Getting married in Thailand
Income $150K	Helping the kids buy a property
	Travelling overseas once a year
	Donating money to charity
	Replacing the car every 3 years
	Taking the kids to Disneyland
	Being fit and healthy
	Not having to worry about money
	Having the latest gadgets
	Not being time poor

Getting from A to B can be difficult and this is where a mentor can really help. A mentor will keep you focused on your destination, and help you to refine your decision-making processes and move more confidently towards your targets. They'll ask questions like 'How will that decision you are contemplating help you get closer to your Point B position?' or 'Is your Point B position still important to you?'

The next chapter explains exactly how a mentor can help.

Chapter 16

A mentor will help you stay on track

'All things are difficult before they are easy.'

Thomas Fuller

Have you ever made a New Year's resolution with your partner to get fit for the new year, only to find yourselves getting home from work on a Friday night weighing up whether to have the pizza and bottle of wine and enjoy couch time or go to the gym?

Exactly – we all have. Where do you think the terms 'comfort zone' and 'comfort food' came from?

You may choose to work with a mentor to keep you accountable on your property investing journey. Your mentor will be there to guide you in the right direction and even introduce you to different ways of investing that you may not have had exposure to before.

Your mentor is there by your side, just like the GPS in your car. If you choose to use a mentor, then they can be like your route guide to success and help you make the best choices along the journey to your Point B position. However, you are always in control of your journey. At any point in time, you have the choice to listen to your mentor's guidance or simply ignore it. If you ignore it and go off course, then your mentor can always work with you to help recalculate your best route back to your Point B destination.

> **Mentor tip**
> Your mentor will challenge you to be brave and make the conscious decision to aim for your goals. Importantly, if you have given them permission to do so, your mentor will also stop you from giving up on yourself.

Remind yourself of your WHY

Your mentor will remind you of your WHY. Why are you even investing in the first place?

It's a simple question but, as I have acknowledged, most people find it incredibly difficult to answer. They may mumble something like, 'Uhh… to make money'. But what does that even mean?

A good mentor will get you to drill deeper by asking you more questions like these:

- How much money?
- And by when?
- And what will you even do with that money if you get it?
- And (most importantly) how are you emotionally connected to that outcome?'

When I ask people to expand on their reason for investing, they may say they want enough money to do whatever they want, whenever they want.

Great! So, what is it exactly that you want to do? And by when do you want to be doing it?

Again, this is where a lot of investors get stumped, because they have never taken the time to work out the exact goals or timelines for all the things that they want to achieve in their lifetimes.

> **Mentor tip**
> Only by asking more and more questions, and getting clearer and clearer about your goals, are you able to start to put together plans to achieve them. But don't panic, I will show you exactly how to do that.

You are the only thing stopping you

There is actually a logical order to my approach to property investing, and about the last thing we need to discuss is the actual property investment itself. The very first thing we need to discuss is YOU. You are the reason why you will or won't build wealth. You are the only thing stopping you right now.

> **#LetsGetReal**
> YOU are the reason you haven't reached your goals.

Can you own up to that fact? Now, I am not saying that to upset you, don't get mad at me, but read that last bit again. You are the reason you haven't achieved your goals so far. The ONLY reason.

Okay, so why is that? Well, this is where it gets interesting.

When was the last time you set goals for yourself? No, seriously – when?

When was the last time you sat down and wrote out your goals, put a date on them, worked out how much cash you needed to achieve them and then committed yourself 100% to achieving them?

Come on now, be honest with yourself. Don't worry, I won't tell anyone. It's okay that you haven't set goals for a while. Most people haven't. We were never taught in school to set goals. Most of us were never taught by our parents to write down everything we want to achieve in life. It does suck, but it's okay. You can start now.

Some of us have only written down goals last year, or the year before, or five years ago. And some of us have even managed to achieve our goals, or at least some of them, which is great.

> **#LetsGetReal**
>
> I can hear people right now resisting this process and thinking to themselves, 'I know what I want, I don't need to write it down!' So, if this is you, go back and remind yourself of the commitment you made to yourself back in chapter 2 about how you were going to cross the lake.
>
> Are you all in or not?

Even if you are one of those amazing people who has achieved everything they have ever wanted, until you have been through the experience of mapping out the next two to five years on paper, in writing, I can guarantee that you will not have covered everything.

Some of the best thought processes happen when your eyes see what you are writing down. One thought leads to another, which leads to another. It's like watching a video on YouTube – you watch one and then you see another, and then you find an hour later you are still on the site looking at cat videos!

Almost like magic, your brain says to you, 'Hey, remember that thing that you wanted to do?' and guess what, you remember something you had completely dismissed months or years ago. Try it. This has worked for me for years, and when you get started it can start a great flow of ideas.

> **Mentor tip**
>
> The best way to do this is to make some time for yourself so that you won't be interrupted by your phone, email, pets or your kids. This is extremely important – make it happen.

For example, when I decided, after many requests, to share what I know about mentoring people to success in this book, I made the conscious decision to travel to Bali to get it done. Okay, getting away from the cold of Melbourne's winter might have been a bonus, but the real reason I did this was because it took me away from my normal routine and distractions. It provided me with clear thinking time.

A mentor is your life hack

> 'The best life hack of all is to just put the work in and never give up.'
>
> Bas Rutten (UFC Heavyweight Champion)

The term 'life hacks' is trending all over the place right now. The success of the term is rooted in the idea that there is some sort of magical series of shortcuts that can transform your results. And in some areas of your life there are no doubt hacks that can make you more efficient.

But perhaps the ultimate life hack is to find a great mentor, or series of mentors, to help guide you through life.

I have only touched on this so far, so now is probably as good a time as any to talk about what The Property Mentors is actually best at: mentoring.

It is not your mentor's job to tell you what to do. The skill, which has taken us many years to develop, is to ask the right questions, at the right time, and in the right order, to help you discover what it is that you want from your life.

Like peeling an onion, we often need to keep opening you up layer by layer until we can uncover what it is that you truly want, and also what you are emotionally ready to achieve.

If you have not identified emotionally with your goals, and if you have not found either a painful enough or pleasurable enough motivation to pull you out of your current level of comfort, then I'm sorry to break it to you but you are unlikely to seriously change your life.

If you don't know why you are doing something, and if you are not strongly connected emotionally to the outcome, then as soon as you hit a speed bump or an obstacle it will become all too easy for you to quit – to give up on your goals and yourself.

And while there is no formal training program or university degree that can adequately prepare someone for a career as a property mentor, all our mentors have been selected and then trained using our proprietary systems, because they have a 'PhD in results'. That is, they have already amassed significant property portfolios themselves and are willing to share their passion for and experience in property with all of our members.

Ultimately, though, given the intensive nature of the relationship, our mentors can only work with a relatively small number of members at any one time.

Who needs a coach?

I want you to use your imagination here for a moment. Let's assume you were the best swimmer in your age group at school. You didn't really need to do any real training, you just happened to have more talent for swimming than all the other kids at your school. Clearly, you knew how to swim and were even pretty good at it, but you decided you wanted to challenge yourself to get to the next level.

So, you entered the regional championships. You figured that because you were now going to be competing against the best swimmers every other school had to offer, it might be wise to do some training. You got up early before school every morning for the next three months and swam laps. Your times improved and you were feeling nervous but confident that you would do okay.

At the regional championship, you swam some of your fastest times ever. You were pretty competitive in most of the events, coming in mid-field in most of the races. In the backstroke event you even medalled – finishing in second place.

But you were not content with that. You decided that next year you wanted to do even better and make it to the state championships. You knew that what you had done so far was not enough, so you looked for a swimming coach to help you get there.

For the next year, the coach helped you to improve your stroke and improve your technique, as well as helping you get fitter and stronger with exercises both in and out of the pool. This coach had you doing things you would never have thought to do yourself, like swimming underwater to build up your lung capacity, training with weights to make your starts and turns more powerful, and even getting regular massages and stretching to keep you flexible and reduce your risk of injury.

Obviously, the better you got, the more specialised and more refined the work that the coach needed to do in order to prepare you to be the very best that you could be.

Our property mentors are your coach

Our property mentors do things similar to the swimming coach in the example above.

Depending on what level you are starting at, they will tailor the work that you, as the mentee, need to do to help take your results to the next level. Their regular feedback and consistent approach will allow you to tweak and tweak and tweak, week after week, year after year, so that you get better and better.

A property mentor will *teach you* and *guide you* through the entire process, and help you to grow out of your comfort zone to get better over time.

By having a mentor, you are accessing other people's experience (OPE). This is a very powerful form of leverage similar to the leverage available when using other people's money (OPM) and other people's time (OPT).

Mentor tip
A good mentor is someone who has done what you want to do and can save you time and money, and the headaches and heartache that they may have experienced over the years.

Your property mentor will help you to assess where you are at currently, both financially and emotionally, and then work in conjunction with you and your professional team (your A-Team) to help you create a property strategy that will give you the best chance of reaching your goals. (You'll learn more about building your A-Team in chapter 18.)

Any property strategy will change over time as you change, and your financial position, goals and confidence do too.

Your mentor will be there with you the whole way through, side by side, holding your hand through the whole process. There will, of course, always be good times and some bad times in life – it can't be avoided, so don't expect a smooth ride all the time or you will be disappointed! – but your mentor will go through these with you so you don't have to do it all alone.

Understand, however, that your property mentor is not there to do the work for you, just as the swimming coach does not jump into the water and do your laps for you!

This is very important to know. If anything, you should treat your property mentor like a good friend – someone you trust and don't want to ever lose. Remember that if your mentor chooses to take you under their wing, then they are making the commitment to help YOU to achieve what YOU want.

#LetsGetReal
Once you have made the commitment to enlist a mentor to help you on your journey, and you give them permission to mentor you, then it is their responsibility to tell you what you need to hear, not what you may want to hear.

Chapter 17

Your three Ds

*'Everything you want is out there waiting for you to ask.
Everything you want also wants you.
But you have to take action to get it.'*

Jack Canfield

Assuming you have big goals and dreams – I hope by now that you are closer to knowing what they are – you are going to have to make some changes to get to that Point B position. Hopefully by now you have committed to doing this, decided to stretch your comfort zones, and mapped out your starting point (Point A) and your goals (Point B).

Now it is time to flesh out your plan for how to best make that happen. While you could do this on your own, as I discussed in the previous chapter, you have the option of seeking out a mentor to help you get better results. Most investors will require someone more experienced than themselves to guide them and keep them accountable.

To achieve your Point B goals, you're going to learn about my three-D approach. The three Ds are:

1. Dream
2. Date
3. Dollars.

They are the three key ingredients to successfully identifying your goals and understanding what you are actually targeting. It's one thing to say, 'I want a house on the beach' (your Dream) but it's another to have a detailed description of the type of house – what it will look like and where it will be located – and know when you want to achieve ownership of this property (the Date) and how much money you need to achieve that goal (Dollars). Then, and only then, will you have something to work towards. Remember, a direct beachfront property was one of my Point B goals, which I achieved by using this exact process. My approach is that once I make a decision to go for all of my big goals, I not only start with the end in mind, I start *working backwards* from the Point B position. I don't just go out there on day one and start investing.

> 'In the absence of clearly-defined goals, we become loyal to performing daily trivia until we become enslaved by it.'
>
> Robert Heinlein

Prioritising your goals

Once you have made a list of all your goals, big and small, you can then start prioritising them by putting numbers next to them. This process will challenge you to start thinking about what is really important to you.

So right now, go and place a number from 1 to ___ (this will vary according to the number of goals you have) beside your Point B goals in order of importance to you. The funny thing is that when I start helping people through this process, I sometimes find they can achieve some of their goals right now – they have just never had the conversation with anyone who can help them to realise that.

Going through this A to B process and working out your three Ds is really quite refreshing for a lot of people.

There is a level of unease when you know roughly what direction you are going in but don't have a clear plan. After going through the process with me, people often realise that it's not material possessions they are after at all. Some people want the big houses, fast cars, yachts and expensive holidays, but when you start drilling into what you REALLY want, why you are really on this planet and what your purpose is, then you might just find that these are not the real drivers for you after all.

> **#LetsGetReal**
> Your thoughts are your emotional drivers that will determine the actions you are going to take, or not take, to achieve all your results in life.

Your life purpose, why you are doing any of this, will become clear when you commit the time to working out your Point B in detail. When you establish your three Ds for each item on your Point B list, you will be able to really add value to the world with more clarity than ever. Once you have this clarity, you will be able to wake up each and every day with a completely different outlook on life.

> **Mentor tip**
> You want to make the world a better place? Take a look at yourself and make a change! I'm not saying you're a bad person, far from it, but making small tweaks along the way and challenging yourself to continually improve will help you accelerate in the direction of your dreams.

Calculating your dollars

Calculating your third D – Dollars – requires knowledge of your earning power and the time you have to left to invest.

Your earning power

Let's do a little exercise here to work out how much wealth you have accumulated so far over your working life. You can do this on paper or, if you haven't already done so on page 98, go to my easy 'A to B' tool on my website at www.thepropertymentors.com.au/myAtoB. There are three steps to this calculation:

- **Step 1:** Add up the value of the assets in your Point A list and then add up all your liabilities. Subtract your liabilities from your assets. The resulting figure is your net worth.
- **Step 2:** Calculate how many years you have been in the workforce (just a rough number is fine – you don't need the months and days, just the number of years will suffice).
- **Step 3:** Divide the figure from Step 1 by the figure from Step 2. This will give you how much net worth you have been capable of creating on average every year of your working life up until now.

```
ASSETS              $1.24M
LIABILITIES         $827K
(worked 23 years)   $413K

$413,000 ÷ 23 = $17,956
```

Now that you have this figure, you have a starting point. This is a bit of a wake-up call for most because it is often an 'oh no' moment. For example, if these were your figures in this example, you would have the earning power of just under $18,000 a year. If you plan on retiring in ten years' time and don't do anything different to improve your results during that time, then chances are you will only have an additional $180,000 to put towards your retirement. That may not be enough for you to live on for the rest of your life.

Many people who do this calculation realise that either they have no chance of hitting any of their goals based on their current position and skill level as an investor, or that they are so far off they need to make massive sacrifices to their lifestyle aspirations or seriously adjust their timelines.

Often, when I go through this process with someone, they realise that what they wanted to achieve is simply not mathematically possible given their current level of investing skill.

Calculating your retirement income

Investors often tell me they want to 'retire' at age 60, or 50 or even 30 with a passive income of $100,000 per annum. (As an aside, what does retirement even mean to you? In some cultures, the word 'retirement' does not even exist.)

How did they come up with that figure?

Most of the time it is just a figure that they pluck out of thin air because it sounds like a cool number, and they figure that $100,000 would be enough to maintain their lifestyle. They have not thought about inflation and the fact that the cost of all sorts of things is likely to go up in the years ahead. Obviously, you can't expect the price of healthcare, food, petrol, insurance and so on to stay the same for the next 10 to 50 years or so that you are hopefully going to remain on the planet. Assuming you own your own home outright in retirement (and not everyone will), to achieve a $100,000 income from your assets you need to know two things:

1. the total asset base you will have in 'retirement'
2. what sort of return you are able to achieve on your assets on a consistent basis.

Let's start with some statistics.

For most Australians, the two biggest assets they will have in their financial lives will be their home and their superannuation. Now, we can pretty much rule the home out because, while it provides you with a roof over your head, it will not produce any income for you (unless you end up having to rent out a room or two to make ends meet).

So, let's take a look at superannuation.

At the end of the 2019–20 financial year, the Australian Taxation Office statistics showed that the average superannuation balance around retirement age (60 to 64) was $357,963 for men and only $287,777 for women.

Assuming you are a married couple with the average balances above, then your total superannuation balance would be just under $650,000. I'll be generous and round that number up to $700,000 so I can make the maths easier to follow.

So, if you wanted to generate $100,000 per annum in income from that asset base, you would need to find investments capable of generating 14% per annum year after year during your retirement, assuming you did not want to start eating into your nest egg.

Are returns of 14% per annum something you have a proven track record of being able to achieve consistently? And even if you have remarkably been able to achieve that return so far, is there any guarantee you will be able to do it in the future?

Let's be a little more conservative then and assume that you could maybe achieve a return of 10% per annum from your superannuation. What sort of asset base would you need to hit your $100,000 per annum income target in retirement? The answer is an even $1 million. But if your ability to invest and still sleep at night means that you are only able to target an average return of 5% per annum, then you would need a cool $2 million in unencumbered assets (outside your family home) to prevent you from eating into your nest egg of savings.

A call out to control freaks

Guess what? No amount of planning will prepare you for all the things that will happen in your life. Over the next few months and years, things will happen in your life that are beyond your control, and I have found that these are the very things that derail the best-laid plans of most investors.

> **Mentor tip**
> Incredible change happens in your life when you decide to take control of what you do have power over, instead of craving control over what you don't.

I will show you later in the chapter that getting from A to B is never a simple straight line. If only it were, achieving all your big goals would be easy. But as the saying goes, 'If it was easy, everyone would be doing it!'

As a mentor, I know that life is going to throw up challenges and curve balls, but not all these challenges are bad. For example, you may get a job opportunity to work interstate for more money, or you may meet the love of your life and now have two incomes (woohoo!).

Knowing we are going to face unexpected events in the future gives us incredible power. It provides us with the opportunity to make decisions about how we are going to deal with those changes, often in advance. We are not saying we know what the changes will be, but rather that we can know what strategies we can apply in response to those changes. (Remember the four-wheel-drive analogy in chapter 13?)

Why investors fail

Most investors fail because, when they are challenged by things out of their control, they lose sight of their end goal – they forget about reaching Point B, most often because their Point B was never properly identified in the first place.

Looking at life logically, though, when something positive or negative (or anything in between) happens, it's tempting to make financial decisions based on what is happening in your life right at that moment.

Here are some examples of positives:

- You get a pay rise at work or win a big contract in your business. Since you have worked hard for it, you feel you deserve to reward yourself and go and buy a new car because the pay rise will cover the extra repayments anyway.
- You get an inheritance or are gifted some money. Given that this was unexpected, you blow it on a holiday, a new wardrobe or some new furniture for the house.
- You sell your house and end up with some extra cash, so you feel you deserve to treat yourself and end up spending it on toys, holidays and other material possessions.

Now let's consider some negatives.

- Your partner gets sick or has an accident and needs to stop work suddenly. You don't have much money in the bank, so you make a snap decision to sell your share portfolio or an investment property to ease the impending financial pain.
- You get made redundant or have your hours reduced at work. Many people think their job is secure when it's not, and this often forces people to make a decision to live off their line of credit on their home loan, and in some cases even live off a credit card, because they assume they will find work again quickly.
- You hear that the property market is never going to improve, or that another disaster like the GFC is just around the corner. Trusting that single piece of information, you decide

to sell an investment property at the wrong time and end up making a loss.

I deliberately left divorce out of these lists because sometimes it's planned and sometimes it's not – sometimes it's a positive experience and sometimes it's not. The two things I know are that 100% of divorces begin with marriage and, no matter which way you look at it, divorces are expensive.

There is nothing wrong with doing any, or all, of the things I just listed; however, most of these outcomes will get you further away from your Point B goals rather than closer to them.

The point I am making here is that in life there are things that can and will happen, and most people let these things affect their investing strategy with little regard for how they are ultimately going to impact on their ability to achieve all the goals they have identified as being important to them.

Obviously, the fastest way to get from Point A to Point B is a straight line. But life is not a straight-line event. In the image below, you will see this represented by the peaks and troughs in the wavy line. The arrows show the points on the timeline where most financial decisions are made. I know that the good times certainly don't last forever, but also the bad times usually don't last forever either. You can usually navigate your way back to somewhere around neutral territory.

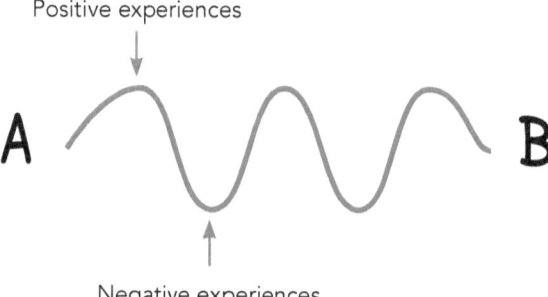

The line between the A and the B could represent a week, a month, a few years or even a whole lifetime. We all know that life won't go perfectly; so, knowing that, let's invest smarter and start making our key life decisions taking our Point B into consideration.

When faced with making any decision, remember to ask yourself, 'Is this decision ultimately going to get me closer to what I am trying to achieve – that is, my Point B?'

By taking this approach, you are already leaps and bounds ahead of most people, who are out there making their decisions based on what is happening in their life at that exact moment.

It's up to YOU

You are the unknown factor when life throws you curve balls. This is why mentoring can be so beneficial. We know that these positive and negative experiences will happen over the course of your life. We also know you will react emotionally, and a mentor will look at the big-picture, helicopter view with you and help you to refocus on your goals.

It is not a mentor's job to tell you what to do, but they will keep you accountable to achieving your goals because you have given them permission to do so and told them that it is important to you. Often a mentor will simply prevent you from making a silly mistake or letting you get in the way of yourself. Ultimately the decision is yours, of course.

We typically allow a two- to five-year timeline for you to get from Point A to Point B, or at least make some good progress. A year is a short time in investing terms; it typically doesn't give us enough time to get that much done. But in two to five years, there is enough time to get you at least heading in the right direction and really starting to get some runs on the board.

This is best depicted in the diagram overleaf, which I call the Control Funnel.

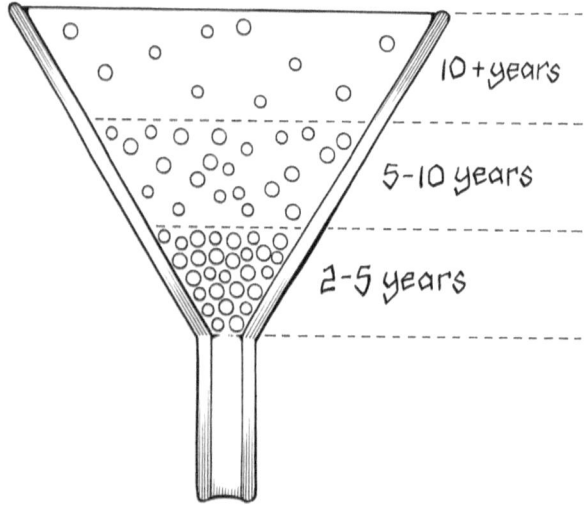

The things in the narrow end of the Control Funnel all collect there and are close by; they are easier to reach and, due to the short timeframe, they are easier to plan. These are the low-hanging fruit in your A to B plan and represent some of the early and easier wins to achieve.

The middle of the funnel is the five- to ten-year stuff; it's a bit further away and there are more variables at play. Your work situation, family life, investment portfolio, health and who knows what else could be different in five to ten years' time. So, what we want to do here is to aim in the right direction rather than dedicate all of our efforts to that one thing. It is important to celebrate as many small wins along the way as possible as well, so that you aren't sacrificing everything for one goal ten years in the future.

Lastly, the wide part of the funnel is the real, big, long-term stuff. These are the end-game goals that you are ultimately working towards.

You want to head in that general direction and, of course, they impact the day-to-day decisions you make around what you do with your available funds – they're ten years away. Now, I know that some people will be saying, 'Guys! We don't have ten years or more'. Well then, that simply means we have a different approach. As with everything we do, there is no cookie-cutter investment strategy.

Chapter 18

Flying to the moon on your own?

'The best teamwork comes from men who are working independently toward one goal in unison.'

James Cash Penney

When investing in property, you need a team of people to help you get amazing results. To fly to the moon requires a coordinated team effort. It is something nobody would ever be able to do on their own.

The book *Team Moon* by Catherine Thimmesh is the story of how more than 400,000 people were involved in the Apollo 11 mission. It provides a rare perspective on a series of events I thought I knew. Apollo 11, the first moon landing, is a story that belongs to many: to the engineers who created a special heat shield to protect the capsule during its fiery re-entry into Earth's atmosphere, to the flight directors, camera designers, software experts, suit testers, telescope crew, aerospace technicians, photo developers, engineers and navigators. It even belongs to the seamstress who put together 22 layers of fabric for each spacesuit!

Having a team of experts is crucial to your success. Hopefully, you won't need to build a team of 400,000 people to help you achieve your goals – but that will depend on the size of your goals!

Most property investors aren't aware of the need to work with a team of experts and they never get their team together. Those who do typically end up with a mismatched group of advisers with the following problems:

1. They don't know what you are trying to achieve.
2. They don't communicate with each other on your behalf.
3. They aren't working on a long-term, coordinated plan for you.
4. They aren't being proactive to help you build wealth.
5. Often, they have never been introduced to each other!

Your team needs to include some or all of the following to help you to succeed:

- accountant
- mortgage broker
- solicitor
- conveyancer
- property manager
- quantity surveyor
- insurance broker
- real estate agent/s
- property valuer
- town planner
- financial planner
- architect/building designer
- surveyor
- interior designer
- pest inspector
- builder

- tradespeople
- building inspector
- and, of course, your mentor!

As you can see, this is quite a diverse range of professionals, all with their own skillsets to assist you in building wealth. Rather than going out and learning each and every one of these professions yourself, I challenge you to think of yourself as the CEO of your own burgeoning property empire.

Your role as CEO

In any organisation, who gets paid the most – the CEO or the worker bees? It is of course the CEO.

But who does the most work, the CEO or the worker bees? (I'm talking about the sort of practical everyday work that is required for a business to be successful – you know, the reception work, the assembly of the widgets on the factory floor, the accounts receivable or the sales for any business.) It's the worker bees, of course.

So, if the CEO is not going to be found in the trenches doing all the day-to-day tasks, then what does the CEO get paid the big bucks to do?

The answer is that CEOs get paid to do the strategic thinking.

The CEO of any organisation is not there to do all the grunt work of the business. Instead, the CEO is there to make sure that all the resources of the business are being utilised to their best ability. Often, the CEO relies heavily on a team of senior personnel for the business to run successfully. The CEO then does the planning and sets the strategy, often in conjunction with the senior management team, to maintain and grow the organisation.

Your wealth team is a group of professionals, whether they are independent of each other or working together in a group, who will be vital to your success. In case you are wondering (and sorry to break it to you), your friends and family are unlikely to be a big part of your wealth team unless they have got some serious runs on the board themselves.

#LetsGetReal
Trying to do it all on your own is rarely going to provide the best results. And even if you had a spare few decades to learn it all, how do you even know if you would be any good at any, let alone all, of the professions listed earlier?

Ask the right questions

> 'An expert knows all the answers – if you ask the right questions.'
>
> Levi Strauss

When an investor wants to buy an investment property, they might go and speak to their existing advisers, or simply ask friends or family for referrals. Have you ever seen a friend's post on Facebook asking for a recommendation on something? That's fine if you are looking for a good hairdresser or want to know where to stay on the Gold Coast on your next holiday, but it's not really the best strategy for building wealth.

I have found the problem is that often these advisers assume that you, the client, actually know what you are doing!

You see, your advisers are paid by you to follow your instructions. So, if you want your tax return lodged, you instruct your accountant to do it for you, and they do it and send you the bill. If you need a loan for a property, great, the mortgage broker will happily aim to get you the best deal available at the time (or the easiest deal for the broker… but that is another matter). But each of these people are simply following your instructions.

If you don't know what you want to achieve, how can you possibly give clear instructions to your advisers?

The majority of the time, unless like a good CEO you are asking the best questions of your senior wealth team, you will usually only get very general advice at best, and poor advice is all too common because you have not instructed your professional team properly.

Advisers generally want and need your business, so they are likely to follow your instructions so that they keep your business. Your team of experts is unlikely to challenge you on your requests and keep you accountable unless you have given them explicit permission to do so.

> **Mentor tip**
> If your instructions to your advisers are poor or vague, then so will be your results. If, however, you give specific and clear instructions, your results will usually be far better. In both cases, you are still going to get a bill for the work they do and the advice they provide.

Cost is what you pay and value is what you get

Many novice investors, and even those who have already purchased multiple properties, don't even know what questions to ask of their professional team. That's okay because that is what mentors can help you to do. An experienced mentor can really assist you to ask the right questions and give clear instructions to your expert property team.

Some new investors realise that they need the professional help, but when it's time to get the cheque book out they baulk at paying for it. I am not saying that everything needs to cost an arm and a leg, but generally you get what you pay for in the property investing space.

Remember, cost is what you pay and value is what you get. Sometimes trying to save pennies can end up costing you pounds.

If you think you cannot afford to use top-level professionals to help you build wealth, then you are possibly not ready to be the CEO of a successful property investment portfolio. Don't take that the wrong way, but without a great team on your side things are almost certain to go wrong.

You will always pay for your education one way or another. Think about that for a second.

I am not suggesting that you will need a $2000-per-hour lawyer when you are just getting started – there are different levels of experts that you will require at different stages of your journey. An investor with two properties will not require the same level of advice as one with dozens of properties across different entities, all with complex loan structures in place.

Sadly, though, even if you have been working with a team of professionals in the past, there is no guarantee that you will have everything structured correctly. I have seen it over and over – when investors have what looks like a successful property portfolio from the outside, once I start stripping back the layers I find that there are hidden minefields that put their entire portfolio at risk.

It's horrible to have to tell someone that there are big holes in their investment strategy, putting everything they have been working towards at unnecessary risk, that will cost tens of thousands of dollars (and in some cases hundreds of thousands of dollars) to rectify.

It's better to get the expert advice at the beginning to avoid this situation.

#LetsGetReal
I cannot fix all your problems but I can promise you won't have to face them all alone.

Expect to be challenged

You need to give permission to your expert team to push back and challenge you if what you are asking them to do for you doesn't fit with your Point B position.

They can only do this if they understand your goals clearly (your three Ds – Dream, Date and Dollars). When they know your goals, they should be doing everything in their power to help you achieve them.

> **Mentor tip**
> If you don't give your advisers permission to push back and keep you accountable, they are unlikely to do it because they want to keep you as a client. They don't want to rock the boat, because they usually have nothing to gain by doing so.

The problem for most investors is that there is practically nobody out there to help you put together your A-Team! It is extremely rare to find someone who not only cares enough to want to help but actually has the specific training, experience and skills to be able to help.

As an investor myself, I have shared in this frustration, which is another reason why I established The Property Mentors. I can now assist people to put together their team and educate them on how to ask better questions.

There are some amazing professionals in each of the fields listed previously, but most of them are there to transact one particular part of your strategy, not assist you with the strategy in its entirety.

Most accountants are not trained to do this holistic work with you, and even if they were, the costs would often be prohibitive at the hourly rates they usually charge. Your financial planner may cover off some of this wealth planning work and may talk about your insurance needs, but in most cases they won't be able to help you with a property strategy, and your mortgage broker will most likely only be able to cover matters related specifically to your ability to borrow.

I'm not in any way discounting the work that accountants, financial planners, mortgage brokers and other professionals in your expert A-Team will do for you – they play a vital role – but you need to know where that help starts and ends. It is a mistake to expect them to do more than they can or should do for you.

Remember, as the CEO of your own investment empire, it is your job to marshal your troops and make sure each one is doing the job they should be doing.

If you are the captain of your rocket ship, you want to ensure the team of experts has done everything in their power to make your trip to the moon have a safe and predictable outcome.

Case study: Dave's gamble on property

Dave currently has a mortgage on his own home and wants to buy an investment property. So, after doing some basic low-level research on the internet about the next boom area, he goes and speaks to a real estate agent and discusses what properties he is after. He then finds a property that fits his criteria and makes an offer.

Feeling good, Dave goes home to tell his partner about the purchase, and she nearly has a heart attack. After buying flowers and chocolates in an attempt to fix the situation, Dave then contacts his bank to discuss the purchase and how he can get finance. (Note that the results may vary with the flowers-and-chocolates approach.)

Already Dave is under pressure because, without understanding the implications, he has agreed to the agent putting a finance clause of only 14 days on the contract. Dave is excited but also nervous as he knows the clock is ticking – fast.

So, the loan application is submitted to the lender and it comes back approved! Hooray! (It is highly unlikely that this will happen within 14 days in some lending climates.) Little does Dave know the bank has 'cross-securitised' his new property with his current home, which puts him at risk should something go wrong. Clueless as to what has happened, Dave and his partner sign mortgage documents and the property settles.

During this time, Dave has been speaking to the agent who sold him the property and the agent was kind enough to pass on his details to their property manager, who will be glad to look after the property. (Real estate agents can also receive commissions of several hundred dollars for referring a new client to their internal property management division – but Dave doesn't know that.)

They find a tenant and the property is now leased. It all seems SO simple, right?

Sure. That seems pretty harmless. There is a chance that Dave may make a profit on his property and possibly reduce his tax, and he may have even bought in an area that booms sometime in the future – but this is not the case for most investors.

Typically, investors may lose their source of income, suffer a few bad years in business, get stuck with a bad tenant, buy in an area that has already boomed, or interest rates increase and the investor can no longer afford the property.

How is this going to help you achieve your goals? Can you see that Dave's approach is more like gambling than investing?

#LetsGetReal
If you are going to the moon, doesn't it make sense to create a plan, attract all the right people to help you and enjoy the journey... and the view from the top?

PART III

WHY PROPERTY?

Remember at the beginning of the book I told you not to flick through to the end where the 'how-to' sections were located? Well, congratulations for reading the first two vitally important parts of the book as I suggested. After reading the chapters up to here, you should have a much better appreciation of how your WHY, your plans and your mindset can influence your success as a property investor.

Now you have made it to the middle of the lake. We're ready to swim quickly to the shore on the other side, learning more of the big-picture concepts regarding property investing as we go.

Chapter 19

So why invest in property at all?

'Real estate investing, even on a very small scale, remains a tried and true means of building an individual's cash flow and wealth.'

Robert Kiyosaki

Have you noticed that we are about 80% of the way through this book and I haven't even really given you any specific technical property information or property-related strategies yet? That is not an accident.

A lot of investors think they need to learn all the technical stuff to become more successful investors. They look for answers to the following questions:

- Where is the next boom suburb?
- Which are better, houses or apartments?
- Where is all the new infrastructure being built?
- How do we achieve the strongest rental yields?
- Where can I find bargain properties?

Now, I am not saying the technical knowledge about how to research, negotiate and secure the right property is unimportant.

It is more that all this technical knowledge comes secondary to understanding how YOU as an investor tick and what you actually want to achieve.

A lot of investors put the cart before the horse when it comes to the order in which they think about and then actually invest in property.

What should come first? Should it be the technical information about a specific property, such as how many bedrooms it has, what type of property it is or where it is located? Or, should you start by working out why you are even investing in the first place and what your specific strategy to achieve that result needs to be?

As you've come this far in the book, I think you know the answer to this question by now.

As I have discussed already, your WHY (your motivation) should precede your HOW (your tactics) which should precede your WHERE or WHAT (your technical research). In other words, the actual property-related technical, or skills-based, knowledge (education) is then just the tool that you will use to execute your strategy.

The Australian love affair with property

Property in Australia is always a hot topic. The property market in this country has always caused – and probably always will cause – a level of excitement, concern, fear and doubt for all of us at some stage. Countless Australians know something about property and most of us seem to have an interest in property, even if that interest involves just watching from the sidelines.

Whenever I meets someone new, I invariably get asked, 'So, Luke, what do you do?' And I usually reply, 'I teach other investors how to make bucketloads of money by investing intelligently in property!'

The very next question is something like, 'Oh, okay, so where should I be buying my next property?'

Now that question in itself is not a bad one, it just comes a few questions too early.

So I might reply with, 'Well that depends – what exactly are you trying to achieve from your next property purchase?' This normally kills the discussion because, as I have said, most property investors don't consciously know what they are looking for from their next, or any, property purchase.

Property is an exciting topic due to the almost endless possibilities that property investment can provide in the long term. To some, even just the short term can make a difference if they see fast growth and are able to time the market. This gives them a rush that they can't get enough of – I have seen it time and time again.

You just have to flick on the TV and check out shows like *The Block*, *Selling Houses Australia* or *Grand Designs* to see Australia's obsession with property. Remember, though, that most of these 'reality' TV shows are far from reality when it comes to real property transactions.

Look out for the bad guys

The level of interest in Australia for investing in property highlights the need for people to get the education first *before* going out there to look for good-quality professional advice. You do need advice but you have to be cautious of who you ask for it. There are a lot of bad guys out there. I use the terms 'sharks' and 'cowboys' to describe those dubious operators who unfortunately tarnish the reputation of the property and investment industry generally.

The cowboys will sell anything to anyone, and they are usually just chasing the highest commission. They will often sell investment properties from glossy brochures, spruiking the features and benefits of the property, such as pools and theatre rooms. They don't usually consider the fundamentals of the investment, let alone take the investor's situation and what they are hoping to achieve into account. Cowboys are blatant in their approach and don't hide the fact they are spruiking and flogging stuff.

The sharks are out there circling, looking for inexperienced investors so they can play on their weaknesses and stitch them up for a property or an investment whether it suits them or not. Sharks are a little more deceptive than cowboys, and they are often slicker and harder to spot, so you need to be careful.

The way I see it, there are sharks and cowboys in every industry, but the door is wide open in the property industry because so many Aussies are so passionate about property. This allows the bad guys to scurry into your life and rush you into signing a contract as quickly as possible. Before you know it, they are gone and no longer taking your calls or replying to emails, and you are stuck with a lemon.

Mentor tip
There are countless property seminars, books, home study courses and marketing companies posing as investment businesses. In the 21st century there are a lot of scams that you need to be careful of. Just google them and find out.

Don't listen to the doomsayers

I have heard a lot of talk, media commentary and, to be frank, a whole lot of hot air in the past few years about what is happening with the property market.

Predictions of serious property price collapses seem to grab the media headlines on a regular basis. Now, I am not claiming that every property in Australia is only ever going to go up year after year. Property still follows some basic economic principles, but it also has some unique qualities that differentiate it from other asset classes.

Lots of bad things have happened in the world over the last 10 to 20 years or so, but still the Australian property market hasn't collapsed! Globally, we have seen Brexit, the Trump factor, the fallout from the GFC, the euro 'crisis', China slowing down, the 'end' of the mining boom, COVID-19, and so on. At home politically, we have had Kevin, Julia, Kevin again, Tony, Malcolm, Scott, Albo and even Pauline back in the Senate – and still the Australian property market has not fallen into some sort of cataclysmic black hole.

'But hang on', I hear you say, 'sure, prices have gone up in the last decade, but they can't keep rising – can they?'

The media is amazing. One day you will read that things are going well; the next day they are reporting a crash! There's plenty of commentary on property, some of it from overseas 'analysts' – often promoting their latest book – or from local expert economists, stock market professionals, financial planners… even accountants and celebrities are asked to comment on the subject from time to time. Wow!

Some of you will remember University of Western Sydney Associate Professor of Economics Steve Keen. Back in 2008, Dr Keen predicted Australian house prices would plummet by 40% from their peak. He's an economist, so he knows what he's doing, right?

Steve Keen agreed to an 'ambush' bet with Macquarie Group interest rate strategist Rory Robertson in November 2008, when the GFC was at its worst. He promised to wear a T-shirt saying 'I was hopelessly wrong on home prices! Ask me how' if his predictions were incorrect. Even worse, he agreed to walk 224 km from Canberra to Mount Kosciuszko while wearing the T-shirt!

I recall having an uneasy feeling about Dr Keen being so publicly humiliated if he was proven to be wrong. And surprise, surprise, he was!

Back then, Australian house prices did dip ever so slightly but they bottomed out at only 5.5% from their peak in late 2008. As Rory Robertson told reporters when dismissing Dr Keen's understanding of the fundamental economics behind Australian house prices, Dr Keen is 'often wrong, yet infrequently unsure'.

Worse than losing the bet, though, was the fact that Dr Keen was so convinced he was right that he sold his Sydney property, a two-bedroom unit in Chalmers Street, Surry Hills for $526,000 in late 2008 after having purchased it for $480,000 in 2006. If you take into account the stamp duty, agents' commissions and closing costs, he likely didn't make much money, if any, on the property.

Had he held on to this property, he would have most likely seen the double-digit growth enjoyed by most of the Sydney property market since then. A search on www.realestate.com.au for two-bedroom units in Surry Hills shows that most recent properties sold for between $1 and $1.5 million. Now, you don't need to be an economist to know selling was probably a poor decision!

Dr Keen is not the only economic commentator to get it wrong over the years.

That house prices did not crash (see Figure 2 overleaf) comes as a great relief for homeowners because, for the majority, property acts not only as their largest financial asset but as a home. In fact, particularly in Sydney and Melbourne, property prices have risen significantly since Dr Keen made his prediction.

So, what should you believe? How do you work out who to listen to and who you can trust?

This book is not designed to dive into all the microdata that is available when it comes to property investing. I will save that for another book. Instead, and perhaps more importantly, I am going to stay focused on the big picture.

#LetsGetReal
Try to remove all the media hype and noise that is everywhere in investment circles and you may just find your decision-making process becomes much easier.

Figure 2: Melbourne Median Dwelling Price 1986-2016

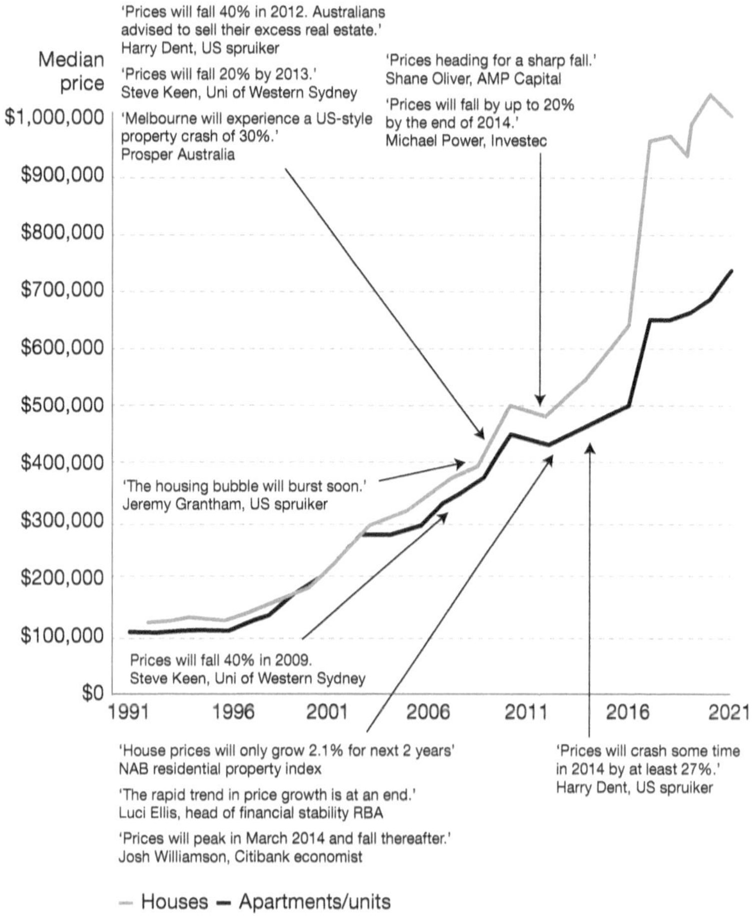

I choose to use Australian property as one of the cornerstones of my own wealth creation plan. The next four chapters explain why. I am going to share with you four key understandings that form the basis of my decision-making process.

Chapter 20

House price stability

*'You get a reputation for stability
if you are stable for years.'*

Mark Zuckerberg

Going right back to the basics, food, water, clothing and shelter are the essentials that we need for survival.

The long-term history of property in Australia is an interesting story. Many of us understand the concept of 'good old bricks and mortar', and the expression 'as safe as houses' certainly has some merit.

However, not all of us are aware of the real data.

According to an August 2022 report by CoreLogic Australia, Australian house prices increased 382% over the past 30 years. In nominal terms this represents average growth of 5.4% per annum.

Did you know that over the past 30 years, properties in Australia have increased in value in far more years than they have decreased – nominally ranging from a high of 17% per annum growth and a low of just -7% per annum?

Were you aware of the fact that just over two-thirds of Australia's residential properties are owner-occupied? And of all the properties in Australia (now getting close to 10 million homes) 32% are owned outright with zero mortgage?

According to data released by CoreLogic to June 2017 (see Figure 3) residential property is by far the largest asset class in Australia, dwarfing the total value of all listed Australian stocks, the entire pool of Australian superannuation and commercial property COMBINED.

Just under 5% of the 9.8 million properties in Australia are traded each year.

To put it into perspective, if one person owned all the property in Australia, they would have around 9.8 million homes, worth collectively $9.6 trillion with a 22.5% loan to value ratio (LVR). In addition, given that approximately two-thirds of all homes are owner-occupied (and hence generate no income), those properties that are available for investment purposes generate around $49 billion worth of rental income annually, according to the ATO's 2020 income data.

Figure 3: Residential real estate underpins Australia's wealth

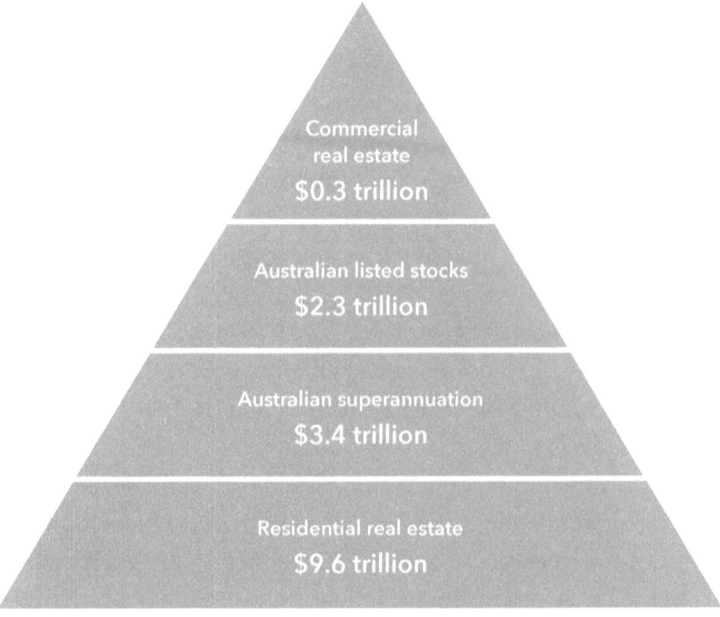

Mentor tip

As a result of serving the primary function of providing shelter to millions of Australians, many without any debt, the property market remains far more resilient to price corrections than many other asset classes (such as shares, gold, bonds or rare art), which are dominated by investors.

Property is in a class of its own

This dual function of property – providing both a home to many as well as an investment vehicle – places property in a class of its own. That's not to say the property market is without risk, or that property prices cannot go down – sometimes they do, and they will do so again in the future.

However, historically, in the face of significant economic headwinds, more liquid assets and assets that do not have the same high barriers to entry (such as stamp duty and legal costs) and exit (such as agents' fees) generally get sold off first. This is because it generally takes an average of 90 days or more to transact a property purchase.

And even then, you still need somewhere to live. You can't live in your share portfolio, raise a family in your bonds or sleep in your gold bullion, now can you?

Perhaps former Victorian Premier Sir Albert Arthur Dunstan said it best when he described just what homeownership can mean to a person. Given this was written in 1943, we can only assume that Sir Albert was referring to all people and not just the men!

> 'Invariably, the man who owns his home is an exemplary citizen. His outlook on life is immediately changed from the moment when the first nail is driven into the structure that is eventually to become "his castle". In reality, it is a symbol of achievement, purpose, industry and thrift.

> The homeowner feels that he has a stake in the country, and that he has something worth working for, living for, fighting for; something he has never had in the past, something he has to look forward to in the future.'

So, it is no surprise that in Australia people still refer to their home as their castle. It is the 'Great Australian Dream' to own your own home. To this day, the majority of homes in Australia are owner-occupied and people still aspire to live in their own home.

The iconic Australian movie *The Castle* highlights how the family home represents more than just bricks and mortar, and how we are prepared to fight and defend our castles. In the movie, for anyone who has yet to see it, a Melbourne family (the Kerrigans) are very happy living in their family home near the Melbourne airport (according to co-writer Jane Kennedy, it's 'practically their backyard'). However, the government and airport authorities try to force them to leave their beloved home. *The Castle* is the story of how they fight to remain in their house, taking their case as far as the High Court. After all, it's not just a house, it's a home.

Just as an aside, in June 2017, the house in *The Castle* was sold to investors and is now available for short-term rental accommodation using the online sharing platform Airbnb. So, for around $220 a night, you too can live like the Kerrigans… if you want to!

People are emotionally attached to property

Not everyone wants to live like the Kerrigans, right next door to a busy airport, and that is the point. Where you live as an owner-occupier or as a tenant is going to be largely an EMOTIONAL decision for most people.

Where will the kids go to school? Where do my friends and family live? Where are the good shops and cafes? How close is it to transport, beaches, work and medical facilities? These are among the plethora of factors that people will consider when they are deciding where to live.

When you attach emotion to something, it takes away a lot of the logic in the decision-making process. Have you ever been to a shop and seen images of a model wearing that stunning dress, or a fit guy wearing some gym clothes, and thought to yourself, 'Hey, if I had that singlet and shoes I would look like that!'? Of course you have – marketing is done that way because companies know it works.

Real estate is no different. Most real estate ads target their market perfectly. Marketers and agents use enticing property headlines such as 'Designer living' or 'Ocean views forever' and there is no shortage of 'Entertainers' delight', all designed to get you thinking about how you can show off your amazing new property to your friends and family.

You are hooked, and come auction time you will do whatever it takes to secure that property. It seems that every weekend I hear tales of how sales prices of one property after another have smashed street records, often going for tens or hundreds of thousands of dollars (or more) above the reserve price.

Now, when buyers start getting emotionally attached to a property, that's when agents and vendors rub their hands together. Two emotional buyers competing with each other for a property is a real estate agent's (and vendor's) dream, as one of them will buy it eventually – it just depends on who has the deepest pockets!

It's never been easy

Do you know any friends or family who bought a property 10, 20 or 30 years ago? Go talk to them, politely ask them how much they paid for it and ask them for the story behind it. Most Australians are only too happy to share this information, and a lot of the time they will have a great story to tell.

As an example, a member's parents bought their first home in the Sydney suburb of Hurstville back in 1970 for $13,500, after putting down a $3500 (25.9%) deposit. Their parents later confessed that this was a huge investment for them at the time, and they only got the loan because they had a strong two-year savings history with the bank.

Anyway, the common wisdom of the day was to work hard and pay off that debt as quickly as possible, and with both of their parents working full-time they dutifully managed to achieve that by 1977. The house was eventually sold in 1988 for $165,000 when they upgraded to the neighbouring suburb of Blakehurst.

This was incredibly stressful, as they committed to buying the new house for $315,000 before they had sold the old house. Back then, they had to take out bridging finance because the first house they were selling took longer than expected to sell back in 1988.

To put some historical perspective around that, 1988 was the same year that interest rates reached 15% per annum, *Home and Away* first aired on Channel 7, Canterbury defeated the Tigers in the NRL grand final and Hawthorn defeated Melbourne by nearly 100 points to win the VFL flag.

With interest rates hovering in the mid-teens, it was a particularly stressful time to take on a new debt much bigger than anything they had experienced before. By the way, that property was subsequently sold in 2013 for over $1 million, so all the stress undoubtedly proved worth it.

#LetsGetReal
Every generation of property buyers and investors has their own challenges to face. Getting onto and climbing up the property ladder has always been an expensive and challenging process.

If you ask people about their biggest property regrets, it is not the ones they purchased but the ones that got away. They may tell you the story of how they could have bought the neighbour's property for a bargain price, or the story about how someone they knew made a bucketload of money by buying property just before a new railway was announced or a rezoning occurred.

I don't deny that housing affordability, or lack of it, is a pressing social and political issue. It's just that every generation has a gripe about the generations before who had it 'easier'.

(As an aside, first home buyers might want to acknowledge that all the roads, rail, hospitals and schools they are using today have been paid for by the taxes of generations that have come before them!)

It is all too easy to listen to the media and accept that property has become unaffordable for first home buyers or first-time investors. If we just use the commonly used median income to median house price ratio as a measure of affordability then, yes, housing has become less affordable over the years. But our population has also grown, and interest rates and inflation rates were, until recently, at historic lows.

Sure, with the Australian median weekly household income sitting at $1807 (that's close enough to $94,000 per annum) according to the 2022 ABS data, and with the median house price in our two largest capital cities sitting at $1,346,193 for Sydney and $964,950 for Melbourne in July 2022 according to CoreLogic, it is easy to think that property is reaching crazy levels.

But so what?

Just for a bit of a reality check, most of the Builders, Baby Boomers or Gen-Xers didn't start out buying median priced properties as their first purchase either. They bought what they could afford, in areas they could afford, and then traded up if and when they could afford it.

For a bit of perspective, previous generations bought homes when interest rates were as high as 18% per annum, inflation was as high as 16.5% per annum and the unemployment rate hit

11% – not to mention some of them had other challenges such as world wars, the oil crisis, the Asian currency crisis, dot.com crashes, the GFC, and so on.

> **Mentor tip**
> Unless you are already on a higher-than-average income, invent the next Google, win the lotto, or fall on a large inheritance, you shouldn't be thinking about buying a million-dollar house as your first property anyway.

I hope my observations here are not offending the 'smashed avocado' crowd. If you don't know what I am referring to, you can read the article written by demographer Bernard Salt in *The Australian* newspaper in October 2016, where he wrote:

> 'I have seen young people order smashed avocado with crumbled feta on five-grain toasted bread at $22 a pop and more. I can afford to eat this for lunch because I am middle-aged and have raised my family. But how can young people afford to eat like this? Shouldn't they be economising by eating at home? How often are they eating out? Twenty-two dollars several times a week could go towards a deposit on a house.'

Bernard Salt's observations caused a massive furore, with many young people up in arms about his comments. Social media erupted, and then 36-year-old property developer Tim Gurner poured fuel on the fire when he reinforced the suggestion that perhaps the expectations of young people were too high when it came to buying their first house. On the TV program *60 Minutes*, he was quoted as saying:

> 'When I was trying to buy my first home, I wasn't buying smashed avocado for $19 and four coffees at $4 each…

My first investment property was an apartment bought for $180k in St Kilda. I spent every night on my hands and knees sanding back the floors, painting, renovating and working on the house. When I sold it, I used the small profit of $12,000 to purchase my next property and it all grew from there. The most important thing for me was just to get my foot in the door at the absolute base level and work my way up from there…'

Perhaps that explains why at age 36, Tim Gurner came in at 157 on the 2017 *Financial Review* Rich List after making $473 million in 10 years.

Let me be crystal-clear – at no stage will I ever say that buying your first property is easy. Not when my grandparents purchased their first home, not when my parents bought their first house, nor when I purchased my first property.

#LetsGetReal
If buying property were easy then everybody would do it, and there would be no need for anyone to own an investment property. Anything worthwhile is going to involve making some compromises and sacrifices.

The gap between property values and wages growth

Let's illustrate the challenges of entering the property market by taking a look at graphs of some key statistics.

First, let's look at the relationship between property values and household incomes over the medium term. We can see in Figure 4 (overleaf) that the growth in real housing prices has raced ahead of wages growth, rents and construction costs since the late 1980s.

Figure 4: Property values in relation to household incomes in Australia in the medium term (2Q86 to 2Q15)

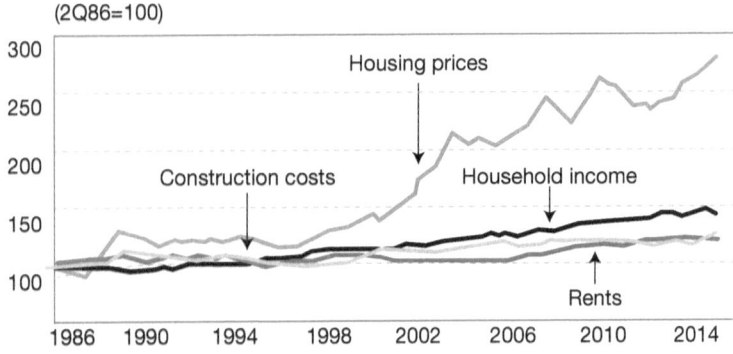

This has been even more noticeable since the early 2000s, when property values started to jump ahead. You can see in Figure 5 how this the gap between property values and wages increased between 2012 and 2016.

Figure 5: Property values in relation to household incomes in Australia from 2012 to 2016

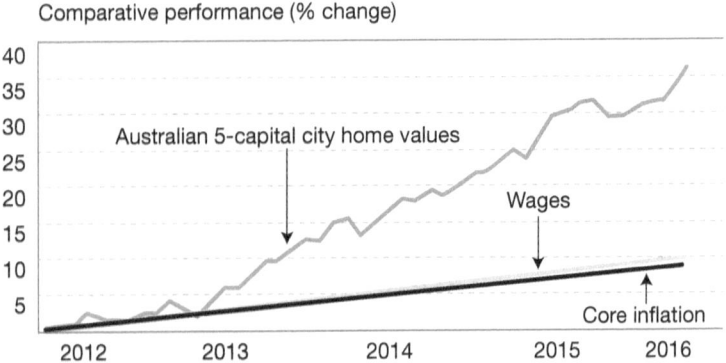

Household debt to income ratio:
June 2012 = 168%, December 2015 = 186%

Increased debt levels

One result of the increasing gap between wages and values is the dramatically higher level of household debt. But Australians still appear to have a strong appetite for property.

Figures show that there was a dramatic rise in investor lending from 2013 (see Figure 6), despite:

- the Australian Prudential Regulation Authority (APRA) tightening investor lending practices by capping the banks' ability to lend to investors
- the banks' own stricter lending criteria
- banks increasing interest rates on investor loans.

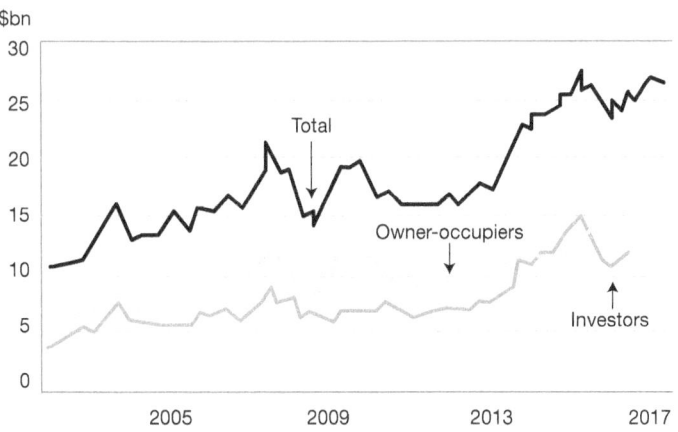

Figure 6: Housing loan approvals

It's important to invest wisely

Ask yourself: do you think property prices are going to come tumbling down, or is it only going to get harder to get your foot on the property ladder in the future if you continue to wait? I think you know the answer and that is why you are reading this book.

> **Mentor tip**
> I see housing affordability, low wages growth and household debt levels dragging on property price growth in the near term. This will make it even more important for investors to do their due diligence and invest wisely to ensure they have the best chance of getting the results they are aiming for.

Now, what I'm going to say here is not meant to be offensive to those of you who are saving hard to get your foot on the property ladder, but please understand if you are trying to buy your first home that you probably will not be in a position to buy a median-priced house in either Sydney or Melbourne. And certainly, your first property is unlikely to be in the inner ring of premium suburbs in one of Australia's major capital cities.

> **#LetsGetReal**
> It's most likely that you might need to live in a one-bedroom unit to start with, or in an outer suburb in a house that is not brand new, without the bells and whistles that you desire.

You may have to make some sacrifices, such as staying at home longer, buying an investment property first, travelling less, eating fewer smashed avocado breakfasts and accepting that you'll be buying a property that is less than ideal. But in time, with the right planning, you should be able to afford to live where you like and in the type of property you really want.

What makes more sense to you?

- **Option A:** Buy your first home (your principal place of residence or PPR), possibly one you don't really love, in an area you don't really like but you can afford, and get no financial assistance with the holding costs on that property. (Additionally, because you will have no rental income, you

will probably only be able to afford to buy the one property for many years to come.)
- **Option B:** Buy an investment property, subsidised by the tenant and potential tax benefits, while you continue renting a better-quality property yourself in an area that you would prefer to live in anyway.

Because of the rental income you receive on an investment property, if you choose option B (also known as 'rentvesting') you may be able to continue buying properties into the future. Plus the chances are, while you are young, you are going to move around a bit anyway, and your property needs are likely to change as you mature and potentially start a family.

> **Mentor tip**
> Just changing the order – buying an investment property first and waiting to buy your own home a year or two later – could make a profound difference to your wealth position over time. Plus, you may actually enjoy a better quality of life to boot.

Why Australia needs property investors

There is an ongoing argument that property should be used purely as shelter and not as a form of investment. Fair enough, but if there are no property investors buying properties and making them available for rent to the general public, who is going to provide the rental accommodation Australians need? The government, you say?

If the government were to step in and become a landlord of the same number of properties that are currently held by private landlords, the financial burden would be immense. The government would have to set up massive departments to source, acquire, manage, maintain, lease and sell these assets over time.

And anyone living in, or waiting for, public housing will have their own stories to tell here.

The government understands that it is not best suited to being a landlord. It is far more attractive for it to offer investors tax benefits to encourage them to provide the rental accommodation Australians need instead. There no simple solution. Any changes to private or public housing needs would have to be introduced over a long period of time. I'm sure you know plenty of people who own their own homes and plenty of people who rent too. Based on that, it's not too hard to work out there is an intrinsic, underlying and unrelenting demand for property for people to both buy AND rent. This is one of the main reasons why I choose to invest in property – there will always be a demand for it regardless of external factors.

Chapter 21

Population growth

'Population, when unchecked, goes on doubling itself every 25 years or increases in a geometrical ratio.'

Thomas Malthus

The second reason I invest in property (after intrinsic demand) comes down to population growth. Population increase can be organic – more Australians having babies – or it can be fuelled by immigration.

Australia has been built on immigration. The immigration history of Australia is believed to have begun with the initial human migration to the continent around 50,000 years ago when the ancestors of Australian First Nations people arrived on the continent via the islands of Maritime Southeast Asia and New Guinea. Fast forward to 1788 and it was the British who migrated to Australia.

A short recent history lesson

From 1852 to 1889 the gold rush in Victoria attracted around 40,000 people from China to Australia. The Irish potato famine saw more than 30,000 Irish migrants land in Australia between 1841 and 1850.

After World War II, hundreds of thousands of displaced Europeans emigrated to Australia, with more than three million people arriving from Europe from the late 1940s until the 1960s.

At this time, Australia believed that it must increase its population to avoid the threat of another invasion. It launched an immigration program, the goal of which was to increase Australia's population, with the slogan 'Populate or perish'.

During the 1970s and 1980s, around 120,000 southern Asian refugees migrated to Australia, including a large number of Vietnamese refugees.

The most recent immigration intakes have less to do with security concerns and more to do with economic concerns. Like most advanced economies around the world, Australia faces such challenges as an ageing workforce, rising pension and healthcare costs, lower GDP growth, increasing sovereign debt levels and budget deficits.

Population growth and its effect on property

Understanding current immigration policy and the reasons behind it can assist us to predict what is likely to happen in the property market in the coming decades, especially on the demand side of the supply and demand equation.

According to the Australian Bureau of Statistics (ABS), Australia's population grew by 418,500 people to reach 26.12 million in the 2021–22 financial year. Net overseas migration added 303,700 people to the population and accounted for almost 73% of Australia's total population growth. This was up from 146,000 in the previous financial year.

Population growth as a statistic in isolation has significant limitations as a predictor for future property price growth – one of which is the timeliness of the data. The most accurate data of course comes from the Census, which is conducted in Australia once every five years. But it takes many months to compile and analyse the data from the Census before we can access the information from it.

> **Mentor tip**
> Population growth is better thought of as a lagging indicator than a leading indicator of property price growth.

Additionally, raw population numbers don't tell us much about the demography of those new Australians. For example, if 400,000 out of the 418,500 new residents were young children, they are unlikely to impact on property markets for decades to come (unless of course we are talking about investing in childcare centres, for example).

The other limitation relates to the fact that just like wealth, population will not be spread evenly across all of Australia. In fact, certain parts of Australia will benefit more than others when it comes to population growth and subsequent property price rises if the supply–demand imbalance becomes affected. As you can see from Table 3 (overleaf), ABS data recorded that the largest change in population growth was in Queensland at 2.2% p.a. on 30 September 2022. This was followed by Western Australia at 1.8% p.a. ahead of Victoria on 1.7% p.a. The other states and territories have experienced lower population growth of between just 0.4% p.a. and 1.4% p.a.

So if, as an investor, you felt that the strong economic and population drivers affecting Queensland might be a good reason to invest for future growth, you might look towards Queensland's capital city for good, long-term growth opportunities. But Brisbane is a big place, and not every suburb – or every house within that suburb – is going to perform the same way.

In Melbourne, for example, *Plan Melbourne 2017–2050* is a comprehensive planning document that outlines the strategies Melbourne will use to house its burgeoning population, which is tipped to overtake Sydney again as the most populated city in Australia by 2032 according to the 2022 population statement from the federal government.

Table 3: Short-term population growth by state or territory

	Q3 2022 ('000s)	Change over previous year ('000s)	Change over previous year (%)
New South Wales	8193.5	108.7	1.3
Victoria	6656.3	108.4	1.7
Queensland	5354.8	114.4	2.2
South Australia	1828.7	25.2	1.4
Western Australia	2805.0	50.4	1.8
Tasmania	571.9	4.1	0.7
Northern Territory	250.6	0.9	0.4
Australian Capital Territory	459.0	6.3	1.4
Australia	**26,124.8**	**418.5**	**1.6**

Clearly, with these challenges also come great opportunities for the educated investor. For instance, it is predicted that over 20% of Melbourne's future growth will be funnelled into just eight local council areas. It might be handy to know where those population growth zones will be and whether that is likely to translate into property price growth in those areas.

#LetsGetReal
One statistic used in isolation of other economic indicators might make great headlines but will rarely help you make wise investment decisions. Also, an investment decision devoid of a thorough plan or considered strategy and not supported by your A-Team will also be unlikely to provide you with the outcomes you really desire.

Now, if you consider that all of these people coming to Australia will need a roof over their heads and a place to call home, this presents massive opportunities for property investors, even if not all of them buy a home straight away. (Some of these people can't help the fact that they are still babies, after all!)

Additionally, affordability constraints and lifestyle choices in what is a relatively young and low-populated country by worldwide standards may see a shift towards future generations electing to, or being forced to, become long-term renters. Now, the fundamental question you need to ask is whether you believe this strong rate of migration, and hence demand, is likely to change in the years ahead.

If people like Dick Smith and others who are against a bigger Australia get their way, the answer may well be no. But how Australia chooses to continue to attract and house its current and future residents will contribute to whether we will see property prices rise, fall or stay the same.

Chapter 22

Property – it's where the money is

'The obvious is that which is never seen until someone expresses it simply.'

Kahlil Gibran

When it comes to investing, the degree of control you have over your assets can shape the type of asset classes you find yourself investing in.

Have you ever heard of Sutton's law? This law is named after the notorious bank robber Willie Sutton, who during his 40-year criminal career stole an estimated $2 million and eventually spent more than half of his adult life in prison. (He also escaped three times.)

It is widely reported – although Sutton himself, in his own book written in 1976, denies ever having said this – that when Sutton was questioned by a reporter as to why he robbed banks, he said, 'Because that's where the money is'.

So, when asked the question 'Why should I invest in property?' I like to borrow the line attributed to Sutton and answer, 'Because that's where the money is'.

As reported earlier, the Australian residential property market is the biggest asset class in Australia, worth around $7.1 trillion.

Now, if you wanted to go out house shopping and found the worst suburb in your closest capital city, then found the worst street in that suburb, and then found the worst house in that street, a number of lenders in Australia are still likely lend you up to 95% of the value of that property (providing you qualify for the loan, of course).

That means that for as little as 5% of your own money (plus stamp duty and legal fees) it may be possible for you to secure a property asset that has the potential to grow in value over time and provide a rental return for the period you control that property.

Now, of course, with recent APRA changes, these days it's more common that lenders will be asking you for a 10% or 20% deposit (plus costs), and will apply stricter servicing requirements, but the point I am highlighting here is that the banks will still lend a large chunk of the money required to help you invest in Australian residential property.

Why is that?

Well, let's stop and think about this for a moment.

Understanding the banks

First, here are a couple of questions:

1. What business are the banks in?
   Answer: Making money.

2. Are they any good at it?
   Answer: They are phenomenal at it.

Australia's big four banks – Commonwealth (CBA), NAB, Westpac and ANZ – make up around one quarter of the entire Australian Securities Exchange (ASX) by market capitalisation.

In Australia, collectively they made almost $30 billion in profit in 2021–22 (see Table 4) and posted collective first half-year earnings in 2022–23 of $16.2 billion. The big four banks also account for around 85% of the residential loans written in Australia.

Table 4: The might of the big four banks

Bank	Net profit after tax ($m) FY22	ASX market cap ($b) FY22	Total assets ($b) FY22
CBA	9595	153.6	1215
Westpac	5281	72.3	1014
NAB	7104	90.8	1055
ANZ	6515	68.1	1086

So, we are not talking about chump change here.

Now, given that the banks make much of their profit by lending to borrowers who buy residential property, do you think they might be able to afford to hire some pretty smart analysts to help them protect and maximise their profits?

Let's put this information together in a logical way.

Using the previous example, if a lender is willing to provide you with up to 95% of the value of even an ordinary property, what does that say about their internal risk-management assessment on that property?

Well, it says that this particular property has been assessed by the banks as being unlikely to drop in value by more than 5% over the near term.

Of course, not all properties will be able to attract such a low-risk weighting. Banks often produce postcode restrictions to lending, or suburb blacklists around Australia, where they are not willing to lend more than 70% or 80% of the value of the property in these areas. Although the banks often don't release current lists, you can google for some historic data.

If you look at these lists, you'll see that in late 2017 regional and mining towns featured heavily, as did many of Australia's capital city CBDs. In other words, the banks were saying that these areas represented a heightened risk for property prices and that they would be discouraging too much activity in these areas by tightening their lending policies.

> **Mentor tip**
> The banks have the ability to either stimulate or dampen investment in any area around Australia via their ability to change their lending policies to protect their own interests. This adds a layer of protection, stability and self-regulation into the demand side of property investment as a whole. Remember, the banks are in business to make money and they are very good at it!

Unfortunately, as an individual investor, you can't impart the same level of control over your own property purchase. Imagine if you had the power to stop other investors investing in the area you just purchased in by tightening access to credit for everyone else.

Factors influencing supply and demand

There are many factors that will influence property prices over the years to come, including population growth, construction of new dwellings, economic prosperity, affordability and financial and government regulation, and they all combine to provide an ever-shifting balance between supply and demand.

> **#LetsGetReal**
> When an imbalance occurs between supply and demand, it almost always results in a price movement that corresponds to that imbalance.

It's vital that you understand this, so let's look at an example. For those who can remember, tropical Cyclone Yasi was a very destructive tropical cyclone that made landfall in north Queensland in 2011. Waves were as high as 12 metres, tides of up to 7 metres above average battered the coast and destructive winds of up to 290 km per hour caused an estimated US$3.6 billion in damage, including decimating the banana crop.

In a balanced market (that is, when supply can meet demand) prices remain fairly constant. So, before Cyclone Yasi wiped out the banana supply, prices for bananas were fairly constant at around $2 per kilogram.

However, after Cyclone Yasi, the supply of bananas was greatly reduced. Demand was not equally affected and, almost overnight, there were far more people wanting to buy bananas than there were bananas to buy – and, hence, prices skyrocketed.

In fact, even though demand for bananas was somewhat reduced as fewer and fewer people were willing to pay $5, $10 or even $15 per kilogram (or more) at the height of the supply crisis, it still took a further nine months for prices to stabilise and for the supply–demand imbalance to return to normal.

The Australian residential property market, like all normally functioning investment markets, works on the same principles of supply and demand. In simplistic terms, if there are more people wanting to buy houses (a demand driver) than there are houses to sell (a supply driver), then property prices are likely to go up, and vice versa.

Banks can influence supply and demand

Not only can the banks impact on the demand-side drivers (via lending or interest rate policy settings), they can also impact the supply-side drivers via commercial lending to property developers.

In other words, if the banks think that prices are rising too fast in any area, and they have concerns about a bubble and subsequent housing price collapse, they can simply make it harder for people to borrow or stop lending altogether, thereby reducing demand. Similarly, if they fear an oversupply of property in an area and the subsequent downward price pressure that follows, they can simply stop lending to commercial developers. This will dry up the supply of new properties until the demand drivers support future price appreciation.

Understanding that the banks will always be driven by their own self-interests and fiduciary duty to provide their shareholders with maximum returns, we can use that information to our own advantage when formulating our investment plans.

Given that the banks are effectively the biggest landlords in Australia, they would prefer to see a steady and consistent growth in property values as opposed to booms and busts. And they have both the will and the means to help influence that outcome.

Government policy affects property markets too

Banks are not the only big players in town that want that exact same thing. Every level of government also has a vested interest in wanting to see property prices continue to grow steadily into the future.

Why is that? Quite simply, it's because property taxes account for over 5% of the $683 billion in revenue a year across federal, state and local government area (LGA) levels (see Table 5).

Table 5: Taxes on property ($m)

Level of government	2016–17	2017–18	2018–19	2019–20	2020–21	2021–22
Commonwealth	0	0	0	0	0	0
State	11,346	12,222	13,790	14,225	14,388	15,638
Local	17,399	18,083	18,904	19,578	20,089	20,840
All levels	28,693	30,249	32,632	33,743	34,411	36,414

Source: http://www.abs.gov.au/ausstats/abs@.nsf/mf/5506.0

Most importantly, property taxes account for almost 14% of total state government revenues and 100% of local government revenues, and it is at these levels of government that the planning of land use takes place.

Property-related revenues are largely related to property values. State governments rely heavily on stamp duty and LGAs on council rates, which are both directly linked to property values.

So let me ask you two questions:

1. Do you know of any state government or LGA that will require less revenue to provide essential services to residents in the future?
2. Do you know of any state government or LGA that can afford to have large fluctuations in property prices from year to year when they are trying to achieve stable budgets?

So, through their approaches to planning, state governments and LGAs can influence both the demand- and supply-side drivers for property.

Each state government produces a state planning policy (SPP), which basically outlines how land can be used for development purposes. In fact, many of the supply-chain restrictions experienced over a sustained period of time in Australia can be put down to inefficient and often expensive planning restrictions.

Equally, the provision of new infrastructure – such as new roads, train stations, shopping centres, schools, parks or other entertainment precincts – or upgrades to existing infrastructure can fuel demand for certain areas.

At a federal level, the government allows you to claim many deductions on your investment property so that you can help them provide rental accommodation for the population. These deductions include depreciation, interest expenses, allowances for repairs and maintenance, improvements and other related costs of ownership – the benefits vary depending on your circumstances. I have already made the argument that the government doesn't want the responsibility of managing hundreds and thousands of individual leases and dealing with tenants, so they allow private investors certain tax benefits for doing so.

So, my third reason for investing in property is because that's what the banks and governments invest in! I go where the money is!

Chapter 23

The ability to add value

'To add value to others, one must first value others.'

John C. Maxwell

The fourth and perhaps the greatest drawcard for many property investors over and above everything already described – and something not possible with many other investment classes – is the ability to add value to property assets. This could be in the form of renovation, subdivisions, rezoning, change of use or property development, to name but a few.

In a world where there are so many things that can spin you out of control, having the ability to control at least some of your investing results via the careful application of your own skill, experience, networks and financial resources is a major appeal for many property investors, including me.

What all of these strategies have in common is that they allow you, the investor, to exert some control over and add value to your property assets. These value-add strategies may help you fast-track your portfolio growth, protect you from market downturns and add valuable cash flow to your overall wealth position. But a word of caution: as with all investing, generally, the greater the returns, the greater the risk.

Mentor tip
While many investors understand the benefits of using these value-add strategies and are attracted to them, not everyone can or should incorporate them straight into their wealth plan. Just because you can doesn't mean you should (which happens to be my favourite saying!).

Case study: First-time developer

I fielded an inbound call recently, and after the normal pleasantries I asked, 'So, Anna, tell me a little about what you are looking to achieve'.

'Okay, I have $100,000 and I want to do a two-townhouse development project', she answered.

'Okay, great, so have you done any developing before?' I asked.

'No!' she replied.

'So, what makes you want to now?' I enquired.

'Development makes me the most money. It is the fastest result and I want you to help me find and complete one of these small-scale developments', Anna responded.

Steady on tiger. I don't even know if I can help this person yet or what she really needs.

'Sorry, Anna, we don't work exactly like that. The first thing we do with all of our members is to get to know what it is they want to achieve from all of their investing. We then work with them to develop a long-term plan that will ultimately help them get the results they want safer, faster and more predictably than if they were to go out and try to do it all on their own', I explained.

'I don't care about any of that. I just want to know how much you would charge me to help me do this development', Anna replied.

I could see where this was headed and wanted to cut it off at the pass.

'Anna, can I ask you a few questions so that I understand clearly what you are asking for here?' I asked.

'Sure', Anna responded.

'Okay Anna, so, imagine you wanted to travel from, say, Melbourne to Sydney. Can we both agree that there is more than one way to get there?'

'Yes, of course', Anna said.

'So, for example, we could do anything from walk, ride a bike, drive a car or fly a plane – would we all agree on that?'

Anna agreed.

'And what you're saying is that you want to take the fastest mode of transportation possible, right? You want to fly a plane?' I asked.

'Yes, that is right, development is the fastest way', Anna confirmed.

'But what you are also telling me is that you don't know how to fly that plane?' I pointed out.

'Oh, but that doesn't matter because my friends and family are going to invest with me. All up, we have $400k for development', she proudly claimed.

'Well, that's different. How many developments have your friends and family done, then?' I enquired.

'None. They are giving me the money and I am in charge of doing the development', Anna excitedly told me.

'Do you mind if I ask how much of the original capital you are all happy to lose with this investment?' I enquired.

'No, we don't want to lose any money. We want to make lots of money!' Anna corrected me.

'Anna, surely you understand that risk and reward are directly proportional? That is, as a general rule, the higher the return, the higher the risk!' I stated.

'What are you saying?' Anna fired back.

'Well, what I am saying, Anna, is that using this analogy, you have told me you want to get from Melbourne to Sydney, and you want to get there as fast as possible. You are going to take your friends and family with you, and they are trusting you to be able to land the plane safely despite the fact that you have never flown a plane before in your life?'

'Yes, I guess so', Anna said, a little less confidently than before. 'Are you saying there is another way?'

'Anna, as we agreed earlier, there are many different ways to get to your destination.'

*

I won't continue with the whole conversation here, but suffice to say I had a long chat with Anna and discovered what was most important to her, why she wanted to achieve those goals and what was both the fastest, safest and most predictable way for her to achieve that outcome.

My point here is that yes, property has the potential for you to add value through renovations, subdivision or more major development, but just because it's possible doesn't mean you should do it. At the very least, do not attempt to do it alone. You need expert help and extras on your A-Team, and it has to meet your Point B criteria.

In the next chapter I look at value-add strategies in more detail.

Chapter 24

There is more than one way to pat the proverbial property cat!

'There's as much risk in doing nothing as in doing something.'

Trammell Crow

Asking me what property strategy you should be using is a little like asking a friend who you should be dating.

As a mentor, I get to know my clients pretty well, and while I might be able to steer them towards a good fit, perhaps even saving them years of pain and hardship, ultimately they are the ones who will have to live with the choices they make.

And just as the perfect property does not exist, there is not one strategy for everyone to follow. So many factors go into choosing a property strategy (or strategies) that is best for you, and it is likely to change over time as you grow and change as an investor.

Don't get me wrong, there are plenty of amazing property strategies out there. One of the great joys in property investing is that there are literally dozens of ways to pat the proverbial property cat. One of my pet hates is so-called experts who only promote one strategy and then try and fit every investor into that mould.

Where do you start?

If you are a novice property investor, or if you've been around the block a few times (pun intended) and are looking to better design your property strategy moving forward, where do you start?

Well, as I have said multiple times throughout this book, YOUR ideal property strategy needs to start with YOU. Ask yourself:

- What are you ultimately trying to achieve?
- Are you looking for a small result or a big result?
- What is your timeframe?
- What knowledge, experience and resources do you possess?
- What does your risk–reward profile look like?

If we assume that you have taken action after reading earlier chapters of this book, then you will have clearly identified WHY you are investing and determined your Dream, Date and Dollars. Now, it's time to think about which strategy is right for you.

> 'In the beginner's mind there are many possibilities, but in the expert's there are few.'
>
> Shunryu Suzuki

First, I'd like to make a point. I enjoy landscape photography and am happy to get out and take snaps whenever I travel. The basics of landscape photography can probably be taught in a single afternoon, and the successful application of all the theory of photography could probably be absorbed within a few weeks. In other words, pretty much anyone could be taking landscape photographs in a relatively short period of time. Some of these photos might even turn out okay.

However, to really achieve mastery over photography to the point where you can actually make a living out of it, have your photos admired by other photographers and have them hanging in galleries or gracing someone else's walls probably takes years of practice, a bucketload of creativity and tonnes of trial and error – and, these days, a massive hard drive!

Just like photography, the basics of property investing can be laid out pretty quickly, but to get truly masterful results probably requires years of dedication to the craft and the application of many different techniques over time.

Each strategy in this chapter could be the subject of a whole book in and of itself. But I give you some pen pictures in this chapter.

Let's start with the most common property investment strategy.

Buy and hold

Whether you adopt this strategy for your principal place of residence (PPR) or an investment property (IP), 'buy and hold' is undoubtedly the most commonly practised investment strategy. With this strategy, you buy a property today and hold onto it in the hope that it will increase significantly in value over time and/or provide you with a rental yield during the time you hold it.

Many property investors start their journey without putting any real conscious thought into the fundamentals of investing. For homeowners, this is fine because they are purchasing property as a home to live in. Their most important considerations are emotional – for example, 'What is the school catchment area?', 'How close am I to work?', 'Where are the shops?' and, 'What's the view like?'

Over time, if they have bought even half well and the markets have risen, they will find themselves with a property worth considerably more than they paid for it. With this newfound equity they might then embark on a renovation strategy, add a second storey or drop in a pool out the back, potentially creating even more value.

So, even though financial considerations were at best secondary when they made the decision to purchase their home, they achieved a good financial result largely by default due to market forces.

However, as with photography, sometimes things don't turn out the way you hope. For a large number of investors, the buy-and-hold strategy has served them exceptionally well, but for others it has caused significant financial distress if they have bought (or been sold!) the wrong property, in the wrong market, at the wrong time of the property cycle or for the wrong price.

#LetsGetReal
The buy-and-hold strategy is sometimes referred to as 'buy and hope', because there are some limitations to the strategy as well as advantages.

When you buy a property with the intention of holding it for any period of time, no-one – and I stress *no-one* – can tell you with precise certainty what that property is going to be worth tomorrow or next year, let alone in ten years' time.

Mentor tip
By doing the right research, negotiating well and being comfortable with some degree of uncertainty, you can load the odds in your favour.

Negative gearing and positive cash flow
Investors choose to buy and hold properties for capital growth and/or cash flow. Essentially, there are two different subcategories of the buy-and-hold approach. Let's look first at negative gearing.

There is a lot of confusion about what negative gearing actually is, how it works, who it benefits and why. But first, what is negative gearing and why is it in the news so much these days?

Using a standard definition of negative gearing is probably just going to further confuse or bore you, but here it is anyway:

> 'Negative gearing is a form of financial leverage where an investor borrows money to invest and the gross income generated by the investment is less than the cost of owning and managing the investment, including depreciation and interest charged on the loan (but excluding capital repayments)…' blah, blah, blah!

Now, just like operating a business or investing in shares, property investing is a taxable activity. Therefore, any income generated or losses made with respect to that activity will impact your income position and the amount of tax you will be liable to pay.

And that is where the confusion starts.

#LetsGetReal
What may be a positively geared property for one person or entity could be negatively geared for another.

It's not the property that determines whether an investment is negative or positive – it's the way that the ownership is structured – for example, in your own name or through a company, trust or self-managed superannuation fund (SMSF) – the resulting tax position and the way you choose to finance the property that determines the final outcome.

The word 'gearing' refers to borrowing money to help you purchase a property. 'Cash flow' refers to the cash position after expenses that the property provides. This can cause confusion for many investors and, of course, those who don't invest and who have a misguided perception about 'greedy landlords' and their negative gearing 'rorts'.

To simplify:

- If a property has *positive* cash flow, this simply means the rental income from that property will cover all of the outgoing cash costs (interest, council rates, body corporate levies, property management fees and so on) associated with that property.
- If a property has *negative* cash flow, this means the rental income from that property does not cover all the outgoing cash costs associated with that particular property. That is, it makes a loss, and this loss reduces a person or entity's overall tax liability.

Adding the word 'gearing' to these terms simply means that the property has been acquired using finance (borrowings) or **OPM** (other people's money) and that interest on the borrowing forms part of the expenses.

To simplify this concept:

- With a *positively geared* property, the *rental income* from that property will be *greater than* all the outgoing cash costs including the borrowings.
- With a *negatively geared* property, the *rental income* from that property will be *less than* all the outgoing cash costs including the borrowings.

To make matters more confusing, a *'negatively geared' property* can actually have *positive cash flow* after income tax considerations have been taken into account for some investors, and after you have taken tax credits gained from legitimate tax deductions into account, as well as 'non-cash' deductions such as depreciation of the building and fixtures and fittings, which will vary from one property to the next.

Confused?

Why do people buy negatively geared property?

Make no mistake about it, leaving tax considerations aside for a moment, a negatively geared property is a loss-making proposition. So, why would anyone choose to invest in any asset that is losing them money?

It's simply because they expect that the value of the property will increase over time at a rate greater than the loss. As discussed previously, Australian property has increased by 382% over the last 30 years according to the CoreLogic report.

This is called 'capital gain' and it's why some people call this a speculative investment strategy. Investors often wait for this capital gain so they can use the increased equity in the property to leverage further and buy more property to build their portfolio.

So, to summarise, negative gearing is when:

- you borrow to acquire an investment
- the interest and other costs you incur are more than the rental income you receive from the investment (in other words, you make a loss – either cash, paper or both)
- you can offset these cash losses and non-cash deductions against income from other sources, which reduces your taxable income and hence the amount of tax you have to pay (compared to the tax you would pay if you didn't hold the investment).

So, why is everyone so up in arms about negative gearing? Well, with inequality rising around the world in response to increasing globalisation, many Australians are finding it difficult to buy a property of their own. So, some people are seeking ways to level the playing field between first home buyers and investors.

Why do people object to negative gearing?

Without going too deep down this rabbit hole, you cannot talk about negative gearing without also talking about the capital gains tax (CGT) exemption, which was introduced in the mid-1990s. In fact, most economists believe that this exemption has had a greater impact on the lack of housing affordability than negative gearing, which has been a part of the tax system since federal income tax was introduced in 1915.

> 'Governments have a tendency not to solve problems, only to rearrange them.'
> Ronald Reagan

The current Labor Government and the Liberal–National Coalition both ruled out making any significant changes to either negative gearing or CGT prior to the 2022 election.

Previously, Labor had set out plans to limit negative gearing allowances to new construction and reduce the CGT exemption to 25% from the current 50% rate.

In July 2017, the Greens released their own policy designed to try and make housing more affordable by taking Labor's now-abandoned proposal and effectively putting it on steroids. The Greens announced that they want to see negative gearing abolished on ALL new property purchases, CGT exemptions wound back to zero over five years and existing negative gearing claims limited to just one property per investor.

For governments, this is a slippery slope. They are trying to make it easier for first home buyers to enter the market and also make it harder for investors to build a property portfolio. But they need to be careful that they don't make it too hard or there may be a shortage of private rental accommodation, putting pressure on an already stretched public housing system and potentially leading to rental increases that would ultimately disadvantage those who rely on private rental accommodation to live in.

Equally, governments must balance, on one hand, the desire to maintain a level of affordable housing for all Australians who aspire to homeownership, and on the other, the desire to take advantage of the undeniable wealth effect that housing can generate over time to reduce their pension liabilities into the future.

Property is the largest single asset that most Australians will ever own. If the property market failed to appreciate significantly over time, then there would be little incentive for anyone to own their own home, or purchase an investment property for that matter (unless rents rose significantly to compensate), and the reliance of individuals upon government handouts in retirement would likely skyrocket.

Obviously, these two desires represent polar-opposite policy objectives. One is designed to keep house prices down and the other to encourage them to rise (albeit in an orderly fashion). Remember, as I have already discussed, all levels of government have a vested interest in property prices continuing to rise.

Who does a buy-and-hold strategy suit?

Firstly, the buy-and-hold strategy suits investors who have some time up their sleeves as, generally speaking, they buy with the view that the market will move property prices upwards over time. This is not a short-term strategy.

The buy-and-hold strategy also has the advantage of being a fairly passive investment approach. Once all the upfront work has been done in researching, securing and settling on a property, the ongoing work may be as onerous as meeting with your property manager once a year to discuss the rent you should be charging, or attending to some basic maintenance issues.

For those with decent incomes now but no (or minimal) assets to their name, it may be desirable to take advantage of the buy-and-hold strategy to start building an asset base that over time will provide sufficient income when they are no longer able to (or want to) actively work for the income to support their lifestyle.

Additionally, and as discussed, under current tax legislation those investors on high personal incomes may benefit by being able to legitimately reduce tax on negatively geared properties. I never recommend that you invest in any negatively geared asset for tax reasons alone, but for some investors the small cash flow loss, with the right property, may suit their long-term strategy, because the main purpose of this type of investment is usually capital growth, not cash flow.

> **Mentor tip**
> If you are relatively time poor and don't have the time to actively work on your property portfolio with all the other things you have going on in your life, this could be a good strategy for you.

Value-add strategies

Again, without going into too much detail given the already somewhat lengthy nature of this book, I will just give an overview here of some value-add strategies available to the savvy property investor.

Renovating for profit

Most Australians are familiar with the concept of renovating property, following the success of TV shows like *The Block*. While much of what you see on reality TV is far from reality, the renovating-for-profit concept is a simple one: you buy an older or poorly designed property and invest in a makeover or significant structural renovations with a view to making a profit after all your costs have been taken into consideration. I have personally completed dozens of renovations over the years – done well, they can make a significant difference to your wealth position. As discussed earlier, the choice of one strategy or another will always come down to a range of both personal reasons and investment decisions.

One of the things many renovators fail to understand is how to appropriately cost in their own time.

I learned this lesson the hard way. Being young and not having much capital to splash around, I decided a hands-on approach to many of my early renovations was the smart way to go. I figured I could save money by doing as many jobs as I could himself. So, every evening after working a full day, and on my weekends, I would drive up to an hour each way to the property to do as much of the demolition, patching, painting, installing and improving to my renovation projects as I could. In some cases, this would go on for months at a time.

It wasn't until, physically exhausted, I decided to calculate what it had cost me to do it all myself. It was then that I realised I would have been better off financially just paying professionals to do the job for me. By the time I factored in the potential loss of income by having the place untenanted longer, and putting a nominal charge on my own labour cost (to compensate for all the leisure time I had missed out on during the renovation period), I discovered that it did not make economic sense for me to have done it all myself.

I was speaking with another renovator recently and we both agreed that if by the end of the project you are not either exhausted, over it or vowing never to do another renovation again, then you are probably not doing it right.

Subdivision

Subdivision simply refers to taking one parcel of land and turning it into two or more titled pieces of land. This can be completed on a small scale by creating two suburban blocks from one, which is known in the industry as a 'splitter block'. Alternatively, subdivision can refer to the creation of thousands of blocks of land in large-scale residential estates, for example.

Whereas a renovation value-add strategy involves hard physical effort, subdivisions are more of a paperwork nightmare.

Wading through state planning frameworks and local council planning documents is not an enjoyable exercise for… well, anyone, I imagine.

Dealing with town planners and local council bureaucrats is extremely challenging. Having to deal with neighbours' challenges and anti-development sentiment can be emotionally as well as financially draining. But obviously, done well, subdivision can deliver big results for those who can see it through.

Property development

Like subdivision, development can be done on a large or small scale. You might start by developing a single piece of land and building a single dwelling on it, and eventually work your way up to developing commercial multi-storey skyscrapers.

Recent figures for developments of different scales are shown in Figure 7.

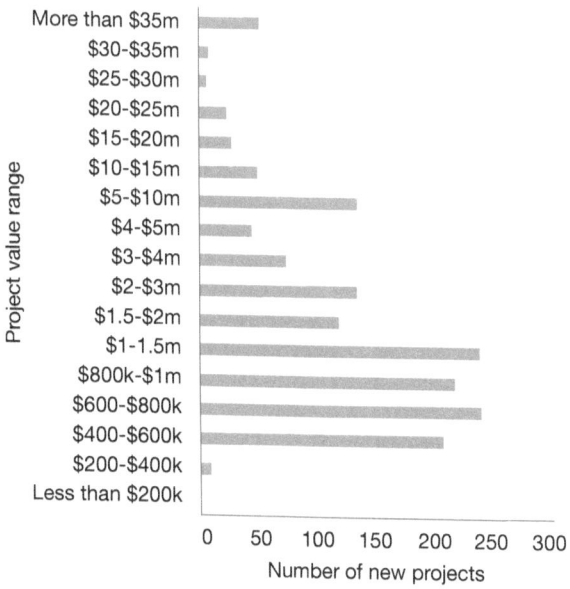

Figure 7: New residential projects

As projects become larger, the rules for property development change, as does the ability to access development finance. The most congested part of this market is found in total project sizes of under $1.5 million. Then the further you go up the project value ladder, the more the competition thins out.

Development takes skill and money

As a general rule, there are five steps to completing a successful property development (see Figure 8).

Figure 8: Five steps to completing a successful property development

Skill	Money	Skill	Money	Skill and Money
Identify, negotiate and secure suitable development site	Adequate upfront capital to secure the target site	Town planning and project management skills to take from concept to completion	Capacity to secure funding adequate to complete the development	Networks to be able to market and sell your development to the end buyer

Step 1: The first step requires having the skills, knowledge and experience to identify and secure a suitable development site. Being able to complete an accurate financial feasibility study for the entire project can make or break your project here. Some people argue that you make your money at the purchase stage of any development, and there is certainly some truth in that.

Step 2: When you have identified a suitable property/site, you need to secure it. In most cases this stage requires a significant cash injection. It is possible to secure potential development sites using advanced negotiation tactics such as property options or joint-venture (JV) agreements, but for most people a significant amount of capital is usually going to be needed to get the project off the ground.

Step 3: Now that you have identified, negotiated and secured the target site, you need to have (or employ someone with) the skills to project-manage the development. If you are buying the site without any plans or development approvals in place, then you will need to run the process from concept to completion. If some of the initial development process was already completed when you bought the property, you may only need to make sure that the construction component is managed well.

> **Mentor tip**
> Project management is not 'rocket surgery', but there are many moving parts and many different trades, government departments and professional services that you will need to be across and manage during the process. In fact, one of the biggest challenges for many would-be developers is that there is a high level of uncertainty that comes as a result of relying on so many people to complete a successful development.

Even the most successful development team can (and probably will) experience delays that are outside their direct control. Not everyone can cope with this stress.

I often describe developing as being like a painfully slow tennis match. On one side of the net is you (and your team), and on the other side of the net are people who may not have the same degree of vested interest or urgency that you bring to the game. So, you might hit the ball over the net by lodging a planning application with the council, for example, and then you have to wait for them to assess the application and hit it back over the net. You might end up in a protracted rally at this stage if you strike the wrong planner, and you might even end up having to change opponent mid-game by taking the matter to VCAT (the Victorian Civil and Administrative Tribunal) or a similar regulatory body in your state. This could drag the game out for weeks, months or even years!

Step 4: Step four scares many would-be developers and prevents most from taking on larger commercial development projects. This is because they need to partner up with a commercial lender who is not only willing to lend them the money for the development project but will do so at rates that are commercially viable. As a general rule, normal residential lending is available for small projects such as a one- or two- townhouse development, but once you start to get into larger projects a whole new set of commercial lending criteria comes into force.

Step 5: Finally, by no means separate from the overall success of the project is your ability as a developer to either market and sell your end product yourself or access the right agents or marketing groups that will do it for you. In fact, a lot of the time the ability to pre-sell a certain percentage of the final properties, or to reach a certain level of debt coverage, is required before commercial lenders will release the funding for the development to proceed.

Risks involved with property developing

As with most of these value-add strategies, the general rule is that the further through the steps you progress, the greater the amount of skill and time you are required to master, the greater the risk you incur and the bigger the potential for financial reward.

So, is property developing risky?

Most people will reflexively answer, 'Of course it is'. Property developers can and do go broke every year.

However, let me ask you another question: 'Are there property developers who year after year are able to generate large profits from developing property?' The answer is, of course, yes. So, when I ask whether property developing is risky, the better response would be, 'It can be'. The risk does not necessarily lie with the strategy itself, but rather with the person or people employing the strategy.

What would be riskier: a first-time developer doing a four-townhouse development or a seasoned developer taking on a 40-unit apartment site?

It's a bit of a trick question because I haven't given you enough information to form an educated opinion. For example, you need to know what sort of markets each is developing in, or what sort of financial resources each is bringing to the table, or how much leverage each will require to complete the development.

This is where a mentor will loop back in and teach you to ask better questions, and over time, through your better questions, you are much more likely to get better results.

Although this is by no means an exhaustive analysis of the property markets, I trust I have been able to highlight some of the big-picture (macro-economic) concepts to consider before you choose to make property a part of your wealth plan.

Here is a reminder of some of the big-picture concepts unique to property investing:

- Long-term stability over 30 years of growth, averaging 5.4% per annum, and resilience to price correction is due to approximately two-thirds of the property market being owner-occupiers and almost one-third of all residential properties in Australia being owned outright without any mortgage.
- Banks and governments have a vested interest in reliable property-price growth into the future.
- Australia has a migration policy that is supportive of future property-price growth (a demand driver).
- You can use your skill and knowledge to add value to property assets.

Chapter 25

Where to now?

*'The best time to plant a tree was 20 years ago.
The second best time is now.'*

Chinese proverb

My final chapter is a bit of a cheat-sheet on how to start investing. In my opinion, these are the ten most important steps you need to take, all laid out for you! Now that you've read this book and are prepared to get real, here are the steps to follow.

Step 1: Make the decision to become a property investor

I know this sounds obvious, but you must make the decision first that you actually want to become a successful property investor. Some people are very good at hoping or wishing that they will get certain things in life. But I am not talking about pipedreams here. I am talking about an unequivocal decision that you ARE going to achieve your life goals. And when I use the term 'property investor', I mean a serious property investor, not someone just doing it as a hobby and hoping it works.

Step 2: Conduct an audit of your strengths and weaknesses

So, if you have made the decision to be a property investor, now you need to get real about whether or not you have what it takes to achieve the results you desire. You need to undertake a complete audit of your current levels of property and financial education, the financial resources available to you, how much time you have, your personality traits and the people currently in your A-Team. If after conducting this audit you recognise that investing the time to become skilled in this area yourself is not your thing, then you will likely benefit from teaming up with someone who has the skill, ability, passion and desire to help you get the results you want. The mentors at The Property Mentors can help to walk you through this process if you need someone to hold your hand.

Step 3: Create your ideal property strategy

Working through the chapters in this book, on your own or with one of The Property Mentors' seasoned property mentors, will help you to create a concise strategy in line with the strengths and weaknesses identified in step 2. Remember, failing to plan is planning to fail. With that said, no plan will ever be executed to the letter, so you need to be adaptable as things happen in your life.

Step 4: Select your A-Team

Even if you have an accountant or a mortgage broker right now, how do you know how good they are? What criteria do you have to compare them against their peers? Not sure?

The Property Mentors can help you by teaching you what questions you should be asking your accountants, mortgage broker or conveyancers and how you can make sure that all members of your A-Team are working together to ensure you get the best results.

We have asked almost every investor we have worked with if they have ever had their expert team on a conference phone call or in a meeting together to discuss their long-term goals. Every time we ask this question, we get the same answer – no!

Most people admit that they wouldn't even know what questions to ask even if that could happen. So, putting all of your experts in the same place at the same time seems like a great idea, and people see the value in doing that, but the reason many investors don't arrange this is because they simply don't want to be the dumbest person in the room!

Your A-Team will need instructions from you on what you want them to do, and if you have never done this before it can be a bit daunting. Having a mentor by your side can take away the barriers to setting up such a meeting, and your mentor can train you in the questions to ask and how to set out an agenda for the meeting. It's all about getting everyone on board with your Point B and your three Ds.

This is an extremely powerful process to go through and gives the whole team clarity.

Step 5: Secure finance and accounting

Working with a top finance strategist and property-savvy accountant can help ensure you not only save money but can safely grow and protect your assets over time. There are ongoing changes in both these industries, and there is no way any individual investor would ever be able to stay abreast of all the changes.

Given that your personal situation is going to change over time, these are two areas that I would encourage you not to shop around for on price. Remember, price is what you pay but value is what you get; you get what you pay for, especially when it comes to your expert team. Again, The Property Mentors can help to guide you through this process to ensure you get the best results.

Step 6: Research your market

Due diligence and market research are an important part of creating the successful results you are aiming for. These skills are beyond the scope of this book, so get in contact with one of the experienced property mentors at The Property Mentors to discover more about how to consistently pick property winners.

Step 7: Source, negotiate on and acquire property

As an individual investor, you are always going to be limited by your personal levels of skill, experience, financial resources and your networks.

Many of the best deals in property are actually off-market. By this I mean they never make it to sites like www.realestate.com.au or www.domain.com.au. Off-market sales are between developers selling to other developers, or real estate agents farming off the best stock to their best buyers before they take it to market. It can save the vendor time if a quick sale is required and may also save them the cost of expensive marketing campaigns.

> **#LetsGetReal**
> Even if you become a black-belt negotiator, you will only be able to negotiate on the pool of property that you have access to.

One of the advantages of working with The Property Mentors is that we are actively in the market and have a vast network of 'property spotters' working for us to help us find the best deals, including real estate agents, solicitors, accountants, financial planners and more.

We get hundreds of opportunities presented to us each month. Our team of analysts runs the numbers against these sites, and only a small handful ever make it through to be considered as being good enough for our members.

Unlike many other property educators, our main focus is on buying property and growing our members' wealth, as well as our own, through specific strategies not commonly available to individual investors.

We work on the principle that by working together we can all access better opportunities.

As a bulk-buying group, we are able to negotiate great pricing, high-value inclusions, excellent purchase terms and many more practical advantages that can make a huge difference to the profitability of every property opportunity we source.

Step 8: Manage your assets

Once you have your properties, it is vital that you have someone look after them properly. Too many investors become disillusioned with property due to poor experiences they have had with bad property managers or tenants.

It is possible to learn what to look for in a good property manager and how to insure your assets to minimise downside risk.

Some investors choose to manage their property themselves to save a few bucks, yet we find time and time again that this ends in tears in one way or another. With so much compliance and legislation to keep up with, you really need to invest a huge amount of time to manage a property properly yourself. Most property management rates are actually quite affordable when you take into account the time, what they have to do and the skills and experience they need to manage what is, after all, often your largest asset.

Step 9: Review and adjust your portfolio

Even the best plans may need to be modified due to unforeseen circumstances. How many people do you know who got crunched by the GFC?

Sometimes you need to be able to adjust your plans, so a regular series of reviews is an integral part of managing your growing portfolio.

Going back to your A to B plan, we know already that your life will have ups and downs in the years ahead. So, instead of reacting and making impulse decisions, conduct regular reviews and make necessary adjustments and tweaks along the way to stay on track.

The other thing to consider is that as you grow and continue to learn, opportunities will open up that you may not have considered previously, and it is highly likely that your dreams and goals will change over the course of your investing career.

Step 10: Enjoy your financial freedom and new lifestyle

The best part is when you get to enjoy the fruits of your labour – the rewards for all the hard work you have put in to build and grow your portfolio.

Property is just one vehicle to help create wealth, which then allows you the time and freedom to do what you really want to do in life.

Adopting an attitude of gratitude, giving back when you can and generally making the world a better place is really what drives us all at a deeper level.

Can The Property Mentors help you?

'A single conversation across the table with a wise man is worth a month's study of books.'

Chinese proverb

Way back in chapter 1, I told you that at some stage as you read this book you would probably come to the realisation that:

- what I have said makes sense
- I clearly know what I am doing
- I have your back and genuinely want to see you succeed in life
- there is a win–win value proposition available to us all by working together.

So, where do we go from here?

Investing in property can be an incredibly lucrative wealth strategy and has served me well over the decades. And while there are many benefits to property investing done well, there is still the potential for you to lose everything if you get it wrong.

To become a successful property investor in Australia, you need a solid commitment to achieve the results you desire. There is no easy pathway to success, and you will need to overcome some huge challenges on your journey if you want to be successful.

Every investor is different and, therefore, what works for one investor could turn out to be a total disaster for another. I have written this book to show you how to get your multi-million-dollar property portfolio well underway, how to keep it and how to live the life you desire as a result.

As you have discovered along the way, this book is simply not another how-to manual designed to teach you all the specific technical skills you will need to thrive in the property investment space.

Rather, this book can be best considered as your 'why-to' manual for success in investing as well as in life. It's a practical manual to guide you through the maze of decisions you need to make to master the property market with the end goal clear in your mind.

But best of all, this book was designed to teach YOU about YOU as an investor, if you take the lessons contained within it on board. If you even just get one tip or idea from this book, or the inspiration to simply get started on your journey, then I have done my job. However, I am confident that you will recognise building wealth does not stop and start with reading this, or any, book.

While it is my mission to continue to help as many people as possible to build successful property portfolios and become financially free, I can only do that for those who are ready to put up their hand and ask for help.

Help can come in all shapes and sizes and, as I have mentioned, if your goals are big enough you will need to enlist the help of many people during the course of your journey. Now is your time to take everything you have learned in this book and get to work, and really build the life you desire.

Make the decision to draw a line in the sand with your life. Start now, because nobody is going to do it for you.

I want you to GET REAL with yourself. All too often people read books, learn a few things and then just sit there with the knowledge and do nothing. But if you are ready to put the lessons in this book to work for you, #LetsGetReal and let's get started.

> **Mentor tip**
> The best time to start your journey to financial freedom is yesterday. The next best time to start is TODAY! If you're not going to do it now, then when do you expect all the stars to line up?

Be honest with yourself about where you are at financially, and if you aren't where you want to be, then do something about it.

While I would like to help almost everyone, the simple truth is I can't.

Like you, I have a finite amount of time and resources available to me.

What we at The Property Mentors build with all our members are long-term, sustainable and *mutually beneficial* relationships. So, whether you choose to work with us or someone else, or continue alone, please understand that the steps outlined in this book, if followed, will provide you with every chance of living a truly amazing life.

At The Property Mentors, we do not charge an arm and a leg for the type of high-quality education, support and exclusive access to all the opportunities that we provide to our members. However, if you can't see the value of working at a real and emotional level, or you want us to do everything for you, or if you are looking for a get-rich-quick approach without making any real effort, then we are probably not the right fit for you.

But if you are looking for a structured, proven system designed to safely help you fast-track your goals, then we will probably be just what the doctor ordered. Whether you are a first-time investor or an elite investor looking to take your results to the next level, we know we can help.

So #LetsGetReal, because when you get real about where you are at and where you want to get to in life, that's when the journey begins.

We look forward to serving you further.

Yours truly,
Luke Harris
Founder and CEO of The Property Mentors

Contact us

To contact The Property Mentors, visit our website:

www.thepropertymentors.com.au.

There you will find information about our one-to-one mentoring program, our online eLearning and our exclusive property investment events.

Praise for The Property Mentors

We first heard about The Property Mentors through my social media. At the time we were going through a vetting process, talking to many 'property experts', and no company was like The Property Mentors. They did not really care how much money we had to invest, but more importantly they were interested in what our goals were. The Property Mentors are very personal in their approach, they care about the dreams and desires our family have and are helping me to achieve them. So, this set The Property Mentors apart from the pack. Another benefit of working with The Property Mentors is the top-class network we now have access to. We have the best accountant, financial planner, property manager – and many more key people – helping us build wealth. It really is a team approach. We are excited to keep working with Luke and the team in the years ahead! *Let's Get Real* is a great way to get an understanding of their genuine approach to building wealth through property and that they are there for the long haul to help you every step of the way!
Emily and Alex Truong, Melbourne, Vic.

I was referred to The Property Mentors by the mortgage broker who helped me secure my first property. My mortgage broker was aware of my property investing aspirations and, based on his experiences, he suggested I look into The Property Mentors to achieve my goals. As always, I was extremely cautious after my first call with my property mentor. Initially, I believed it was 'too good to be true'. It took me a number of open conversations before, six months later, I decided to take up one of the strategies on offer.

I have taken on a few more strategies since then; one has been completed and a number are in progress, but I have had a taste of the results and they are very promising.

I would describe The Property Mentors as a collective – all of whom are interested in using property investment as a means to secure a fulfilling and happy lifestyle. The mentors are all experienced and trusted advisers who take a keen interest in how their property investing strategies can work within your means and current financial commitments to achieve your life goals. I cannot speak highly enough of my property mentor and the time and effort he has put into helping my family and I create an exciting plan for our future.

Tegan Denyer, Moura, Qld

We met The Property Mentors at an investment seminar around three years ago. The topics they presented were of great interest to us, as we had started our investment portfolio and wanted guidance from people who were experts in their field. They helped us with our plan and put forward questions we hadn't even thought about. We put our goals down on paper and started discussing what we would like to achieve.

The Property Mentors have improved our investment journey, and we have been able to achieve real results that are a vast improvement on those of previous years. Having a mentor there to oversee, educate and guide us, rather than just tell us what to do, helps us to understand and make better decisions. We have introduced our children to the team so they can get some exposure and education on an alternative way to reach their investment goals. This has opened their minds and they have started to realise what is achievable.

We regard Luke and the TPM team as friends; we appreciate all they have done for us in the past and what they will do for us in the future.

Stephen and Joanne Sciberras, Canberra, ACT

I first got involved with property over 40 years ago, when I bought my first property with my mum. Since then I have bought and sold a number of properties and have used property as a vehicle to build assets for my retirement. As part of staying abreast of developments in the market, I used to go to whatever seminars were on offer, and that is when I first heard Luke speak. He was very passionate, knowledgeable and committed. More importantly, he had more on offer than just buying property – he spoke of a range of strategies to make money out of property-related investments. I was impressed and checked him out, and his associates and his company, and I have now committed significant funds to their strategies.

The Property Mentors opened up a range of strategies that appealed to us as we changed our investment portfolio approaching retirement. They have worked closely with us to evaluate options and, more importantly, have proactively assisted in their implementation. There are many players in this market, but I know of no others with the range of strategies and the organisational structure that positively assists members achieve their goals. Their approach to risk management is second to none.

Membership is not cheap but payback on the investment was virtually immediate. Luke and our mentor have had long sessions with us to refine our goals and develop strategies to best meet them. They have worked. No one else has ever given us the time and commitment that we have received from The Property Mentors. No one else has the range of options and level of support.

John and Donna Gibbons, Bundeena, NSW

Luke 'does' property investing with genuine integrity, significant skill and dedication to doing the right thing by his members. He has a ridiculous eye for detail and deeply understands that wealth creation is driven by your mindset. If you want to begin or improve your wealth-creation journey, then avoid all the expert 'noise' and sit quietly with this little gem *[Let's Get Real]*. He is in this with you, for the long haul. On retirement, Luke's 'rocking chair test' will be to ask himself, 'How many souls did I positively impact?' Will you be one of them?

Enjoy the read!

Greg Smith, Nunderi, NSW

Let's Get Real is a great read for anyone wanting to build up the knowledge and confidence to really change their results. *Let's Get Real* is also a fitting description for my personal situation, after having spent a number of years in a relationship that just wasn't working for me. After much deliberation, I had to make the difficult decision to dissolve my marriage. As a result of the divorce and subsequent settlement, I walked away with only a small amount of capital to invest. But that money has to serve me and my daughter for a lifetime, and I was highly motivated to ensure that my financial future was secured.

As a health care professional, I have spent years studying and building real-world experience in my profession, and I am highly competent and confident in that space. However, when it comes to investing, I recognise that I am not an expert. Thankfully, I was introduced to Luke and the team at The Property Mentors. I have to admit I was nervous at the start, but their approach is unlike anything I had experienced before. As true mentors, their approach was genuine, caring and considered. I never felt like they were trying to 'sell' me anything or had anything but my best interests at heart. Over a series of in-depth conversations, they really took the time to identify what it was I wanted to achieve. This approach is certainly something I would never have taken on my own, and the process even uncovered some things I didn't know I wanted and certainly had no idea were even possible.

Anyway – long story short – their approach, their professionalism, their experience and their genuine desire to help provided me with the initial confidence to start investing. I will also admit that until I received that return on my first investment, I was still a little nervous and had to trust that it would all work out OK. It did and since then I have continued to invest with The Property Mentors as we work towards creating my 'Point B' position (see chapter 15).

I am eternally grateful for their support and guidance and am only too happy to recommend The Property Mentors to anyone looking to take their results to the next level.

Melissa Loercherer, Melbourne, Vic.

I finally feel like my financial future is now secure, thanks to the support and guidance from Luke and the team at The Property Mentors. I am a young, single mother trying to financially rebuild after a lengthy and expensive divorce. Left with limited funds and without a home to raise my family in, I needed help and direction on where to go from here and how I was going to get there. This is what initially attracted me to The Property Mentors.

Through their mentoring, Luke and his team have guided me through a process of self-discovery. They have helped me identify my goals and how I can best achieve them. I have been asked the hard questions, rediscovered my WHY and learnt how to best start over.

I am confident that I am now moving forward towards a more positive financial future for not only me but my children as well.

Although I will admit that I found this process very confronting, I know I wouldn't have been able to make better investment decisions without it – or them. In return, I have been rewarded with the education and knowledge to enable me to make smarter investment decisions moving forward – not decisions based on short-term thinking or quick fixes, but rather decisions that suit my long-term agenda and are backed by solid research. Despite still being at the beginning of building my property portfolio, I have full confidence that Luke and the team will be right behind me, supporting, educating and guiding me every step of the way.

Alisha Guest, Melbourne, Vic.

Initially, I attended a seminar where The Property Mentors were giving a presentation. I was very impressed with their knowledge and passion for property investment. It made me realise how little I knew about investing in property, which prompted me to seek out The Property Mentors' expertise. I have now been investing with The Property Mentors for over two years and feel very well supported and part of the group. Luke has been very flexible in accommodating my investment needs, nothing is too much trouble and I feel more than 'just another client'.

It's great that Luke is prepared to help others by putting his experience and knowledge into a book.

Ron Miller, Harvey, WA

Luke is so easy to talk to, it didn't take long for me to feel comfortable enough to open up and trust him. He is very supportive of me, my personal goals and my ambition to be a professional property investor. Luke has a wealth of knowledge and experience, which is why I joined The Property Mentors – I'm new to investing and need the expertise. With Luke as my mentor, I've learnt to be brave, trust the process and enjoy the journey of self-discovery whilst reaping the rewards that come with owning property.

Belle Bollinger, Sydney, NSW

Working with The Property Mentors over the last three years has been a fantastic and rewarding experience. Our mentor has introduced us to investment strategies to suit our goals and provided us with excellent support and guidance at every step of our property journey. We always knew that a large part of our success would be dependent upon working with the right team, and we are so fortunate that we have The Property Mentors working by our side as we progress towards achieving our financial goals. We would highly recommend The Property Mentors to anyone who is serious about taking control of their financial future. The team's knowledge, support and expertise continue to surpass our expectations, and we are looking forward to working with them for many years to come!

Stephen Smith and Kelly McManus, Melbourne, Vic.

Being an ambitious 25-year-old working in the construction and property industries, I thought property investing would be easy – simply save a deposit, jump online, visit a few display suites, attend a few auctions and, finally, once you find something that you liked, you just buy it, right? To my ignorance, saving the deposit was the easy part.

No, [property investing] is not easy; rather, it's the opposite. You discover a whole new list of emotions and quickly realise it's a whole new ball game, working up the courage to throw your life's savings down on a property you won't be living in and hoping it will be a successful investment.

After searching the internet and doing the above for six months without success, a family friend encouraged me to call The Property Mentors to assist. So, finally getting over my ego, I contacted them. The following month, I attended my first Mentor Masterclass. The Property Mentors changed my whole perception of property investing with their approach to first surround yourself with a team that can support you and ensure you purchase the 'right' property – the 'right' property being one that suits your personal financial situation and long-term goals. My mentor facilitated the entire process from go-to-whoa, while taking the time to ensure I was comfortable and understood each step along the way. The Property Mentors' collaborative approach gave me the confidence to purchase my first property in late 2016. Since then, my best friend has also purchased an investment property with the support of The Property

Mentors. I'm glad I have The Property Mentors in my corner and have confidence I purchased the 'right' property that suits my Point B goals.
Matt Pellegrino, Melbourne, Vic.

I love the way The Property Mentors have set up their property education. They start from the beginning and go ahead step by step, not only covering property but also other aspects of property investing, like goal-setting, finance, accounting and structures. Above all, their support is second to none. Having access to a mentor has made a big difference, as initially my property goals were unrealistic. Working on my strategy with them has shown me how to do things and keep it real, which I appreciate.
Ravi Shah, Melbourne, Vic.

Our journey as members [of The Property Mentors] has been an immeasurable ROI. We have gone from dreaming to making our goals a reality. The education provided has enabled us to take action with confidence. We are very grateful to have a mentor who can actually help us achieve the success we want because she has already achieved it!
Noah Pacey, Perth, WA

My mentor has been wonderful, providing guidance through areas in my portfolio which I found, personally, very difficult to resolve. I am a homeowner and also have had one investment property for over ten years. Since The Property Mentors have been mentoring me, I am much more confident going forward with further investments.
Preston D'Laroy, Melbourne, Vic.

Although my relationship with my mentor is still quite new, he has already helped me in clarifying my goals for the short, medium and long term. In saying that, I truly feel like I have a mentor behind me who can help me achieve these goals. The Property Mentors' approach is not to hold my hand and tell me step by step what to do, but rather empower me with the knowledge and education I need to build long-term wealth whilst also acting as a guide along the way. To use an old proverb as an example, their approach is definitely about teaching a man how to fish, rather than catching fish for him. They have not tried to sell me any property, upsell me any products or be pushy in any kind of way. Their wealth of knowledge in all aspects of property and development

is evident in the way my mentor presents the right opportunities to me based on my situation whilst also giving me the knowledge to reach my own decisions. I know I have found a team that is in it for the long term and is truly invested in assisting me and my family in reaching our goals.
Jason Sas, Melbourne, Vic.

I've known Luke professionally for more than ten years. The tools and personal experiences that he shares in the book highlight the dos and don'ts in property investing and how important it is to have a good mentor who will work alongside you to [help you] achieve your financial goals in life. *[Let's Get Real]* is a great read, and I would personally recommend this book to anyone who is considering investing in property for the first or a subsequent time.
Mario Vinaccia, Melbourne, Vic.

Absolutely love it *[Let's Get Real]*! [The book] got me in right from the start. It really questions whether you are ready or not to do what it takes to get the results you want and tells you it's going to take some change. It's got just the right amount of 'truth hurts' and yet inspires you to want to be better and know more. I always enjoy a good quote and Luke has chosen a good selection from a variety of people.

Luke has shown us a wealth of out-of-the-box strategies that we could never have been exposed to had it not been for his flair, ingenuity and contacts. He is ethical, generous and above all an honest, good guy.
Tony and Glenda Moore, Duncraig, WA

As a financial planner, I have been working with The Property Mentors for some time now. They take a unique approach to property investing that I haven't seen in a property investment firm. They provide property investment solutions that are focused on ongoing education and mentorship of the clients they work with. This not only sets them apart but ensures that clients continue to add to their knowledge base whilst investing, which continues to increase chances of success over the long-term investment journey.

This has shown me, and continues to show me, that they not only 'talk the talk' but 'walk the walk' in creating a win–win situation for all.
Mark Pearson, Melbourne, Vic.

Also by Luke Harris

Once you've gotten real, it's time to get *Property Fit*!

You don't start jogging by running a marathon, and you don't begin weight training by lifting 30 kg dumbbells. There's a process to getting into shape and achieving peak performance.

Investing in property is the same. You need to start by learning how other people invest – including the mistakes they make. You have to find a team of experts (your 'trainers'), do some self-assessment (your 'fitness test') and then start to look at how you will achieve your goals.

Property Fit assists you with all of this. In this easy-to-read, practical book, Luke Harris helps you find an investing strategy that fits your ultimate goal of financial freedom.

Available from all good bookstores and at majorstreet.com.au

For more information, visit thepropertymentors.com.au

www.ingramcontent.com/pod-product-compliance
Lightning Source LLC
Chambersburg PA
CBHW020353170426
43200CB00005B/159